Will's Journey

Will's Journey

(Angels of the Appalachians Book 3)

Deanna Edens

Will's Journey
(Angels of the Appalachians Book 3)
By
Deanna Edens

Cover Artwork by akinshin@DepositPhotos
Photo of Will and Pearl by art-siberia@DepositPhotos
Will walking to the cemetery by nature78@DepositPhotos
Books with quill by photomaru@DepositPhotos
Photo of Hank by vivienstocks@DepositPhotos and Tessy by
kipuxa@DepositPhotos

ISBN-13: 978-1542617741
ISBN-10: 154261774X

Acknowledgements
Special thanks to Nancy Holloway, Barbara L. Jones,
Pam Tindell, Geneva Lacy, David Robert Edens Jr., and
Ella Bokey for providing editing advice.

Some of the anecdotal illustrations in this book are true
to life and are included with the permission of the persons
involved. All other illustrations are composites of real
situations, and any resemblance to people living or dead is
entirely coincidental.

This story is a work of fiction.

Other Books by Deanna Edens

The Convenience of Crafting Maple Fudge
Welcome to Bluewater Bay
Christmas Comes to Bluewater Bay
Mystery in Bluewater Bay
Love Blooms in Bluewater Bay
*The Adventures of the Bluewater Bay
Sequinettes:*
The Complete Bluewater Bay Series
Angels of the Appalachians
Molly's Memoir
Erma's Attic:
Angels of the Appalachians Book 2
Rosa's Castle
Jinx at the Greenbrier

"For Will and Pearl"
(And all angels of the Appalachians)

"Feathers are reminders that angels are always
near."
– Jamie Lee Loga

It has been proposed that Shakespeare's original accent would be more akin to the Appalachian dialect than to any other vernacular in the world today.

I can't assure that this is true, but I do know I have always been especially proud of the folksy phrases and artfully amusing adages, which are uniquely our own.

It is virtually impossible to capture the eloquence of this language in the written word, which is why you should call on the wild and wonderful folks of the Appalachian Mountains to experience it firsthand.

Angels of the Appalachians

Angels of the Appalachians is a fresh and endearing tale, filled with folksy phrases and amusing adages of the South. It's the story of two women who meet in 1980, gray-haired Erma telling her life story to Annie, a young college student living in Charleston, West Virginia. The tale she tells is also of two women, and their adventures beginning in the coalfields of Red Ash, growing up near Thurmond, and eventually finding their way to Charleston in 1915.

Strong mountain women, historical places, faith, and grief are themes explored in this account of a friendship that spans across decades.

You will find yourself wishing to call on the fine folks of the Appalachian Mountains, relax for a spell, and stumble upon the angels who made West Virginia so gloriously wild and wonderful.

Erma's Attic (Angels of the Appalachians Book 2)

When Annie, a young doctoral student living in Charleston, West Virginia, takes the advice of an elderly friend and spends a few nights at a farmhouse up Black Hollow Road, she discovers a journal in the attic.

The aged diary, she soon realizes, was written by her dear friend, Erma, who had recently passed on over to the sweet by and by. Her friend's memories transport her on an adventure that defines and embraces involvement in the women's suffrage movement, chatting with Mary "Mother" Jones, and standing vigil outside collapsed coal mines in the first half of the twentieth century.

Tales from the past, and from the present when the

journal is uncovered, are woven together to ultimately offer readers a compelling picture of life in the West Virginia Appalachians.

Now, let's move on to Book 3 of the Angels of the Appalachians series—I hope you enjoy *Will's Journey*.

"What in the tarnation are ya doing up there, Annie?"

"What?" My grip tightened around the sagging narrow trough that was flimsily attached to the roof. I peeked down only to see Will staring up at me. His hand was covering his eyes in attempt to shield the glaring sunshine. "I'm cleaning out the gutters. They're packed full with leaves and maple tree helicopters. It's hard to tell how long it's been since these have been cleared."

"Those aren't helicopters," Will corrected me, "they're called whirlybirds."

"Whatever you call them is fine. I just know the maple tree has been dropping them like crazy."

"Why don't ya hire someone to do that for ya after all the leaves have dropped this fall?"

He carefully balanced his cane before he bent over, plucked a feather from the grass, and tucked it into his pocket.

"I'm broke, Will." My attention turned back to the task at hand. "I can't afford to pay anyone to do the chores around this old farmhouse." I purposefully dropped a fist full of dried *whirlybirds* on his head.

"Do ya need a loan?"

"No," I took in a deep breath, "I start to work on the twenty-first and will get paid the week after. Right now, I have enough money to pay the bills."

He quickly diverted the conversation. "It's not a very smart idea to be climbing a rickety ladder, Annie. Ya might fall off and break a leg and there's nobody here to help ya. Aren't ya nervous being up there so high?"

"I wasn't until you planted the thought into my head," I sarcastically countered.

"I still don't think it's wise to be climbing a ladder when nobody's around."

"Hank's right there." I pointed in the direction of the snoozing hound dog.

"What if ya fall and can't get up?" Will slid his Mail Pouch from the pocket of his overalls.

"Hank would go fetch help. He's a smart dog."

My fearless comrade lethargically opened one eye before rolling over and covering his face with his paw.

"Where do ya figure he'd go to fetch help?"

I shrugged my shoulders. "I don't know, maybe down the hollow to Henderson's farm?"

"What if Mrs. Henderson isn't home?"

"*Seriously?*" I measured. "I don't know, Will. Maybe Hank will just go in the house and dial the sheriff's office."

Will let out a barely audible grunt before pinching out a wad of tobacco and sliding it into his jaw. "Ya know, Annie, sometimes I think you're a fairly smart girl and at other times I think your cheese has done slid off your cracker."

"Thanks, Will."

"It wasn't a compliment."

I suppressed a groan. "What are you doing up Black Hollow Road this afternoon?"

"I brought ya up some groceries from the store and I have something I wanna run past ya."

I started descending the ladder, which triggered Will to rush over and steady the wobbly wooden rungs. When I was safely planted on the ground I inquired, "What is it you want to run past me? It always makes me nervous when you brainstorm, because it usually means that I am involved."

We sauntered around the house toward the large wraparound porch and dropped down onto the decaying plaid couch that was situated beside the front door. I noticed three large paper bags, propped by the screen door, filled to the rim with a variety of groceries. "Will," I informed him earnestly, "you don't need to give me food. I really am doing fine with money."

"Those aren't for you. They're for Hank." A high-pitched whistle escaped his lips. When Hank heard the shrill toot he came running to Will's side. My old friend tugged a slice of beef jerky from his pocket and dropped it into Hank's wide-open mouth. Will's eyes darted around the porch, "Where's Tessy?"

"I'm not sure. I saw her a little while ago."

Hank butted Will's knee with his nose and steered our attention to the gap underneath the couch. Will leaned over and snapped his fingers, "Come here, Tessy." The tiny cat tripped out from underneath the couch with dainty steps. Her broad green eyes stared up at Will as he fumbled around in his side pocket ultimately producing a tuna flavored tidbit.

"Ah," I nodded knowingly, "you brought treats for everyone, I see."

"Yep." He handed a Twix bar to me.

"Thanks, Will. Twix are my favorite."

"I know." He spat a mouth full of dark, thick liquid into the neck of an empty Coke bottle.

"Why do you always bring us our favorite delicacies?" I asked.

"Annie, when I was growing up my family was dirt poor; actually we were so poor we couldn't afford dirt." Will laughed at his own joke before continuing, "My father died when I was young so my mama took up cleaning and ironing for the rich folks 'round town. There was one lady named Mrs. Jackson, who was fairly well to do, and on the days my mama cleaned her house Mrs. Jackson would pay her and give her a small box of chocolates. Now, Mama could have saved those three pieces of chocolates for herself, but she never did. She would bring them home and give each of us children apiece. Mama always told us she didn't care much for the taste of chocolate and it wasn't until years later that I learned how much she really did love it. Ever since then I try to keep the things I know people love close to me so I can brighten their day." He shrugged dismissively, "Plus the love I give returns to me."

"That's very thoughtful, Will," I acknowledged. "So," I nudged him as I ripped the corner of my candy bar open, "what do you want to run past me?"

"Run past ya? Oh, right. Did ya know that Pearl Chandler had a son named Jonathan who passed away a few years back?"

"No."

"Well, she did. He was almost fifty years old when he died and he was autistic."

"Really?"

"Yep."

I waited for Will to continue.

"So, Pearl has been visiting Buster Thaxton a couple of times every week and she has decided to see if the State will allow her to be his caregiver."

"She is... is volunteering to take care of Buster?" I stuttered hesitantly.

You see I had met Buster Thaxton earlier in the spring when I was outside the farmhouse cleaning up the fallen limbs left over from winter storms. He just about scared the bejeebers out of me when he suddenly appeared from nowhere. Hank had leapt onto his shoulders and knocked him to the ground. After I telephoned the sheriff's office, Sheriff Holmes arrived and arrested him. Although Sheriff Holmes insisted he was a wanted criminal I suggested he may have a special condition, and sure enough, we found out Buster is autistic. "That's very honorable of Pearl, but is she sure she can handle him?"

"Yep," he twisted on the couch to face me, "I'm going to help her."

"Help her," I reiterated.

"I'm movin' into her house."

"You are going to live *in sin* with Pearl Chandler?" My voice rose in volume, "She's the choir leader at The United Methodist Church, Will." I regarded him disbelievingly. "This will prompt people to gossip about her all over Sissonville. She'll be the talk of the town and not in a good way, I can assure you."

"I asked her to marry me, Annie."

My mouth gaped open. "You asked Pearl to marry you and you didn't tell me?"

"I'm tellin' ya now."

"You barely know her, Will. You've only been dating for... for how long? A month? Don't you think you're rushing into things? Remember, only fools rush in where angels fear to tread." I recommended unsolicited advice, "If you've fallen in love at first sight, you better look twice."

"Annie," he replied in an overly consolatory tone of voice, "Pearl and I are both approaching ninety years old. We don't have a lot of time left for sparkin' an' spoonin'. Plus, I've been very lonely since my wife, Lillian, passed away... and then Erma died... a man my age needs to have a woman in his life."

My finger started waggling in the air. "You told me one time to never test the depth of the water with both feet and now you're jumping straight into the lake!"

"I'm not jumping into nothin'. When I'm with Pearl I'm as comfy as an egg under a hen sittin' in a wool basket."

"Geeze," I shoved a bite of Twix into my mouth.

"Annie, I'm an old man. I know what I'm doing."

"Truue," Hank chimed in.

"You too?" I snarled in the direction of the old hound dog. "You always take Will's side."

Hank kindly responded by spraying me with slimy slobbers when his head energetically shook, *"Nooo."*

"Yes, you do." I informed him sternly.

"Would ya quit fussin' with the dog and hear me out?"

"Fine," I scowled, "let me warm up some lunch and you can tell me all about this well thought out plan of yours."

"Okay." Will balanced his cane on the floor and hoisted from the couch.

"It is very well known that I can make a rockin' pasta dish," I told him as I handed over one of the bags of the groceries he had brought to me. I cracked open the screen door allowing Will, Hank and Tessy to enter and held the door open with my foot as I stumbled into the living room balancing the remainder of the groceries in my arms. Dropping them onto the countertop I informed Will, "Hank has a tick. Would you mind?"

"Mind what?"

"To yank it off him. You know I'm afraid of ticks."

"Where's it at?"

"In a place where I'd rather not stick my fingers."

He glimpsed down at Hank. "Do ya have a tick, old boy?"

"Tikkk," the dog corroborated.

"Where's it at?"

Hank ambled over to Will, crooked his head to the side, and used his paw to direct Will's attention to the precise location of the decisively attached culprit.

"Oh," Will sniffled, "that is a foul location."

"Yes, indeed," I agreed.

"Can I borrow your tweezers?"

A disturbing visual flashed through my mind's eye. "The ones I pluck my eyebrows with? I don't think so."

"You can disinfect them later, Annie."

"I could never use those tweezers again if you pluck a tick off of Hank's butt with them, Will."

"Women," I heard him mumble under his breath.

He walked to the kitchen door, opened it, and tossed something on the ground.

"Did you get it?"

"Yes, Annie. I got it."

Will settled down at the kitchen table as I lifted a few cans of pasta from the cupboard that was stocked with Chef Boyardee's Beefaroni, Spaghetti and Meatballs, and Beef Ravioli. "My specialty," I told Will as I presented him with the choices.

He specified the ravioli with an outstretched finger.

I was emptying the second can of ravioli into a saucepan when a booming belly laugh, filled with mirth, erupted outside the kitchen window, which triggered Hank to yelp out a piercing warning. I peered through the pane glass, only to see Pearl Chandler bent over and curiously probing underneath the barn door.

"It's Pearl," I informed Will.

"Pearl?"

"Yes." I opened the back door that led into a sloping field with a grassy bank and ancient, log barn positioned about twenty yards away. Will and Hank nearly ran over me as they whizzed toward the dilapidated outbuilding. I followed behind them and soon we were all peeping underneath the narrow gap separating the barn floor from the ground.

"I'm sure I saw a mother cat with a kitten in her mouth dash under here. The kitten was just a tiny little thing. It was as cute as a button."

A minute later we were all lying face down, scanning the dark, restricted, weed-covered area.

"I see something over there." I aimed my finger toward a large piece of wood where I believed I saw a terrified little blob of black crouching in the corner.

Hank wriggled in a little further.

"Do ya see anything, Hank?" Will asked.

"Nooo."

"I haven't seen any cats around here," I said, "other than Tessy, of course."

"Ya should keep your eyes open. Evidently, you have one wanting to move in with ya."

"Great," I thought, *"that's all I need. More varmints to take care of."*

"We've probably scared her. She won't come out now," Will announced as his creaking bones slowly unfolded and he lifted himself from the ground. "Hank will keep an eye out, right ole boy?"

Hank started enthusiastically nodding his oversized head. Suddenly he turned his nose up, sniffed a couple times, and scurried toward the kitchen door.

A plume of pungent smoke wafted in the air when we stepped into the kitchen.

"Oh, no!" I swiped up a dishcloth and lifted the charred saucepan from the gas stove. I dunked it into a sink of sudsy water, causing it to sizzle on impact. Grabbing a metal spatula, I scraped the burnt bits of pasta stuck to the bottom of the pan.

"I thought it was very well known that you could make a rockin' pasta dish," Will teased as we fanned the smoke looming in the air.

"Peanut butter and jelly sandwiches it is," I apologized.

"I brought ya up some bologna and white bread," Will said as he began removing miscellaneous articles from the brown paper bags.

I spun around to face him. "You said you brought those up here for Hank," I reminded my friend as I dried my hands on a threadbare towel.

"Well," he smiled, "Hank is a generous ole dog and I figured he'd share 'em with ya."

"Right," I replied, embarrassed that Will felt like he needed to buy me food. I sliced a few pieces from the hunk of bologna. "Does anyone want this fried? I can make a rockin' fried bologna sandwich."

"Nooo," Hank pleadingly intoned.

Pearl provided a petite shake of her head indicating that she wasn't interested in having her bologna fried.

"Absolutely not!" Will fanned at the smoke-filled air circulating around us. "I occasionally enjoy a good old raw bologna sandwich."

I sliced off a hunk of bologna for Hank before we finally settled in around the table with *uncooked* bologna and mustard sandwiches, potato chips, and glasses full of RC Cola.

"Let me tell ya'll a joke I heard yesterday," Will said as a sly grin spanned his face. "This young couple got married, and she was kind of nervous cooking her first dinner. She fixed up a big pot of beans and served her husband up a big plateful. He ate awhile and then she asked him how the beans were. 'They're pretty good,' he said, 'but I believe they are a little burned.' Well, she said, 'Them beans are not burned!' She got mad and they had a big fight over whether or not the beans were burned. They got so mad they didn't speak to each other for two weeks. Finally, one day she came down and said, 'I'm sorry for getting so mad. Let's make up.' He said, 'You're right. It was silly to get so mad over those burned beans.' " Will started chuckling before he spit out the punch line. "She said, 'Them beans were not burned!' "

Pearl, Will and even Hank started cackling out loud and I joined in fully realizing Will was trying to lighten my sour mood after the ravioli incident, which had left a foul-smelling reek swirling about in the kitchen.

Pearl finally blurted out, "Did you tell Annie the news yet, Will?"

He nodded, took a long sip of cola and cleared his throat. "Well, I haven't informed her of *all* the details."

"Details?" My eyes zipped to Will, then to Pearl, and back to Will again.

Pearl grinned, reached over and patted Will's hand. "We were hoping you wouldn't mind if we held our wedding ceremony up here at the farm. I love the view of the mountains from your front porch and since we are getting married next month we decided this would be a splendid place to tie the knot. It puts me in mind of God's country." She sighed romantically. "Plus the trees should be flaunting their finest shade of scarlet leaves in October."

"Next month?" I glanced at Will.

"Yep." Will dipped his chin in confirmation.

"Fools rush in," I mused, before I came to my senses. "Of course!" I finally stammered. "Absolutely!" I stood up and walked over to hug Pearl. "I am so happy for both of you." I

smacked Will hard on the back. "Just thrilled."

"Good," Pearl replied, "you won't need to do a thing. We'll bring all the food and it will be a small ceremony. We're only inviting around twenty people."

"I won't have to do anything? I'll just need to pick up every single stick, dried-up walnut shell, and broken limb in the yard, dust the furniture, mop the floors, shine the windows, and buy a new couch cover to disguise the layer of dog hair that is permanently caked into each thread of fabric, then drag the old plaid couch from the front porch and find a place to dispose of it."

My mind started racing. I felt my heart palpitate just thinking of the chores that would need to be accomplished in the span of one month. "This is so exciting." I squeaked out.

"Yes," Pearl smiled, "we're really excited too."

"Well," my hand rose to cover my heart, "all I can say is congratulations."

"Thank you."

With a fixed smile plastering my face I asked, "When is the big day?"

"October the third."

"Less than a month." I gulped.

"Yep," Will elucidated, "we decided the third would be a perfect day. It's a Saturday, it's my birthday, and it's the same exact date that the angel rescued me when I was in the Army."

Pearl's eyes grew wide with excitement. "Will, tell her about the first time the angel rescued you." She shifted in her seat to face me. "This is a heartwarming story, Annie. You're going to love it."

"Less than a month?"

Bluefield, West Virginia
June 21, 1901
Broken Arrow
{{2}}

"Come up here and look at this, Will." Josh motioned with his hand.

The little boy climbed into the loft of the barn and stared out the tiny window. He saw before him the widest stretch of water he had ever viewed. From his vantage point, the river widened the broad lowland and curved away between its bluffs to empty into a blue-green, slow-flowing stream that appeared to be about a quarter mile wide. Never had he seen such a beautiful or mighty river. It was so wide that its far bluffs looked blue and they were covered with dark, dense forest and brilliant green grass.

"What's that river called?" Will pointed out the window.

"Elkhorn Creek," Josh replied.

"That's the biggest creek I've ever seen."

"Yeah, it's as wide as a river."

The Van Dyke farm was the finest land Will had ever seen and he felt fortunate to be spending the week with his cousins, Mary, Gina, Grady, and Josh. Every morning and evening they'd have a big meal sitting around the table with everybody jabbering all at the same time. He didn't see Mary or Gina much, and Grady, being the oldest son, was usually helping his father out with chores around the farm, so this left him alone most of the time with Josh. Josh was ten years old, which was two years older than Will and he sure enough looked up to him.

"Do ya know how to catch a rabbit?" Josh asked.

Will thought this through before answering, "Nope."

"The way ya catch a rabbit is to hide in the briar patch and make a noise like a carrot."

Will started laughing. "That's a good one, Josh. I'll have to remember it so I can tell the fellas at church."

"Do ya know how to shoot a bow?"

Will, naturally, guessed another joke was coming so he replied, "No, how?"

"Ya don't know how to shoot a bow? What's wrong with ya? Are ya stupid?"

Will was a bit taken aback, but finally responded. "I thought ya were going to tell me a joke, Josh. Of course I know how to shoot a bow. I can shoot an arrow 'bout ten yards."

"Do ya want to go hunting? I know where Grady's bows are. We could head over to the edge of our property line by the river where there's an old pile of rock covered with lichen and moss. I know the deer usually come out a little before sunset to graze around."

Will shrugged his shoulders. "Sure. Why not?"

"Wait for me here. I'll go fetch two of Grady's best bows and some arrows. I'll be right back."

When Josh returned he handed a weapon to Will and they set out toward the bank of the river.

"We're going to *still* hunt," Josh explained, "the deer are used to me sitting and watching them so they ain't scared of me. When they come down off the hill it will be easy to shoot them 'cause they'll be real close."

"Okay."

The boys found a place to settle in and silently waited. Will could see the stream glittering under the sinking sun. A soothing and gentle river breeze hushed over the whole valley. It wasn't no time until several fawns came out of the forest, cautiously stepped nearer and began grazing in an open space not more than ten yards away.

Josh motioned for Will to shoot first, so he drew his arrow from the quiver, nocked it and set himself in an archer's stand. He consciously chose the largest of the fawns.

Luminous eyes gazed at him with utmost calm.

Extending his left arm, he tightened it around the handgrip, then pulled his right hand toward him, sighted the fawn along his shaft, and released firmly. *"The bow bent in a perfect arc,"* he proudly measured.

The sound of the bowstring was that of a sharp twang accompanied by a muffled crack. The arrow went through the fawn's chest wall, half its length. *"Most likely a mortal wound."*

"Good shot, Will!" Josh shouted out.

The fawn ran, thrashing about toward the protection of the dense forest. The faint cry of distress caused a doe to come out of the forest, seemingly to protect her young. As the herd scattered frantically through the forest the boys followed behind.

They followed them into the thick forest and came to an open knoll in the woods, deep with ferns, giant oaks, cedar and pines. Heaving with exertion, Josh plopped down on the ground. "We best be getting home for dinner."

"What 'bout the fawn?" Will pointed up the hill. "Shouldn't we track it and make sure it's dead? Drag it down so we can eat the meat and tan the hide?"

"Nope, we ain't supposed to be hunting this time of year and don't tell my dad we were either. You can't mention a word of this to anyone or we'll get our butts blistered."

Will felt sick at his stomach. He could see, in his mind, the fawn's eyes trustingly staring back at him. "But... "

"Let's go, Will." Josh started walking down the hilly

path.

By the time they made it back to the farmhouse, they could hear the call of coyotes in the far distance now.

"Most likely thinking of food," Will cringed, *"of having a feast."* He fought back the overwhelming need to throw up throughout supper and when Mr. Van Dyke suddenly asked, "You boys ain't been out shooting deer, have ya?" his stomach lurched.

"No, sir." Josh lied.

"Good," Mr. Van Dyke stirred his stew, "we're not in need of any meat right now and you know we don't shoot deer this time of year."

"I know," Josh replied. He kicked Will underneath the table.

Later that night, when everyone was asleep, Will stood at the bedroom window staring out toward the river. The sight of the fawn's eyes kept rolling over and over in his mind. He felt ashamed. The moonlight revealed a towering line of grim clouds crawling in from the Southwest. Thunder grumbled, lightning flickered on the horizon, and the clouds climbed high. He quietly descended a flight of stairs and propped open the front door. Standing on the porch he felt a blast of damp shiver through him, and he noticed the leaves in the yard had turned white side up. Soon the rain came and it lasted all through the night.

Downpours of rain continued to pelt down throughout the following day, and the river rose at alarming heights. Mr. Van Dyke and Grady walked down and checked it every few hours to access the potential for flooding. The Elkhorn, which fed numerous basins, was swelled in an hour into a roaring gush of water.

At around midnight that night, Will snuck out of the house, and even though the rain was pouring down, he stood, getting soaked in his pajama bottoms, for a long while at the brushwood field that led into the woods. He stared up the hilltop and wondered what had become of the young deer. He walked across the field and gazed into the dark forest. Lightening flashed, thunder roared, and the rain came down in torrents.

He could hear animals all around him running up the hillside. They were everywhere—to his right, to his left, in front of him and behind him. He could distinguish their steps in the rustling brush as they scurried away from the water ominously gushing below him. The river suddenly sounded so close.

He squinted back and could see the dark waters rapidly rising. The creek banks had swollen and covered the path he had taken and now there was no choice but to climb higher up the mount. He followed the wild animals ascending the slippery slope through the maze of trees, rocks, roots and brushwood.

Will pulled himself up the steep hillside by roots, rocks and shrubs, pausing every twenty feet or so to hug the slopes and breathe with his face against the ground until he could raise the strength to go on a few more yards. Nearly an hour later, when he reached the peak of the hill, the boy stumbled upon the hulk of a great beech tree that had long since fallen. Its center was rotted out, leaving a cavity some two feet wide. It was lying on its side and floored with the soft decay of drifted leaves. He dragged his drenched body in, rolled over so his back was facing the opening, and eventually passed out to the deafening clatter of rain.

That night Will dreamed of sassafras tea, and of how he and his mama would go up to the sassafras clump above their cabin after the spring thaw had softened the ground, and pull up the aromatic roots and shave them into the tea kettle to boil for a spring tonic. His mama would add some maple or cane syrup to sweeten it. He could smell it; the way it steamed... he abruptly woke to the sound of the drumming river and could feel the tree shell, where he had found refuge, shifting erratically beneath him.

Disoriented, he rolled over and lifted his head above the edge of the beech hulk. He immediately realized that he was surrounded by water. *"Had the river flooded the whole valley and soared this high up the hill?"* He had no idea how deep the water encircling him was, but when he saw a fawn's head, its eyes milky and tongue gray, floating a few feet away from him, he cried out in anguish.

The fawn, its flesh half eaten from his hind end, appeared to be caught in the high brush. The dark swift water rushed by it causing it to quaver, as if in tune with the rhythm of the swirling overflow. He could see a fragment of an arrow thrusting out of the fawn's chest wall. A bolt of dread snapped throughout his body, his scalp flushed with prickles and his heart seemed to jump up into his mouth. He blinked repeatedly, eyes streaming tears, and lips quivering as he gawked at the crumpled fawn.

Will hugged himself, trembling fiercely, and tried to recover his breath. "Help me. Somebody help me," he whispered. "I'm sorry."

"Don't be afraid." Will heard a majestic voice intone through the hiss of the falling rain.

He looked toward the heavens where a powerful figure soared above him. The shape glistened, radiating; an orb surrounded the angelic form, protecting it from the downpour.

"Be still," the angel spoke.

Stunned, Will stared at him for a long moment before

finally murmuring, "Alrighty, then. Thank ya."

The angel's strong hand seemed to reach down, covering the boy in a protective embrace and gingerly nudged him deep into the protective walls of the beech where he remained all that day and into the night. A single feather drifted down and the boy stretched up and clutched it in his hand. He examined it carefully and wondered why it was still dry—still able to glide through the downpour of rain.

Will's stomach rumbled from hunger. His throat was raw and there was an arid dryness in his mouth. Every time he glimpsed over the edge of the hulk, he could see the rotting fawn's cloudy eyes staring back at him, then he would open his hand and stare at the feather. He finally was able to prevent his body from trembling and drifted in and out of a disturbed and fitful sleep.

Early the following morning, he felt the water beneath him gently stirring. It felt as if the whole vast river was now subsiding, and then it seemed to quicken. He peeked out, only to realize he was caught in a narrow rushing stream. Wedged inside the wooden barriers he was plummeting down the mountain, caught in an overflow of murky water rushing down the steep hillside. He could hear thumping noises as he rolled over debris and felt the jolt and thuds beneath him as his decaying sanctuary hurried over rocks and roots, finally colliding against a massive oak tree. He took in a deep breath to gather his courage. Slowing bending at his waist he pushed himself up and took in his surroundings.

He screamed out in terror.

Only a few feet away there was a perpendicular, jagged rock cliff. The thick muddy water was gushing past him and pouring over the edge down into the river below. The mangled fawn was wedged between two oak trees. Its lodged body was preventing the beech hulk from tumbling over the sharp vertical overhang. The force at which the water surged inhibited him from escape.

"Be still," the angel once again addressed Will.

Will focused heavenward and saw the mighty angelic form hovering above the edge of the cliff face. "Okay," he whispered.

Quickly recognizing he would be swept away in a second, should he attempt to wade through the turbulent gush of water, he jerked his knees up to his chest and curled up into a tight ball. He prayed and wept, then ardently prayed some more. During these long hours, he could think of virtually nothing but of how much he missed his mama and of the careless manner in which he had shot the fawn.

Finally, a little before sunset, a dull rose glow began to burnish the bluffs across the seething river. Great rents opened in the purple clouds above the western horizon and glowed scarlet. The storm receded across the river making an enormous backdrop for a perfect rainbow that seemed to straddle the river. The angel had disappeared and the waters had diminished. Will could hear a faraway thump of horse's hooves. He rose from his hunkered position and trundled out of his shelter. Will shouted, "Help me! I need help!" His voice was weak and he doubted it could be heard.

The footfalls became louder and he could feel them now through the soaked ground on which he lay.

"Help!"

"I think I hear a voice," a man shouted.

"Where?"

"Over there."

"Here! I'm over here!" Will screamed with all the force he could muster.

"'Tis a child," the man yelled as he approached on

horseback. He tugged left on the bit collar in an attempt to redirect the horse before slowing down its gait. The mare blew softly, took two steps backward, and then halted.

Two other men followed closely behind. One man pointed to the fawn and said, "Ain't that the darnedest thing ya ever seen?" The twisted fawn was tangled and knotted within tree limbs, branches, and thick brushwood that had formed a blockade, comparable to a beaver's sturdy dam. The crisscrossed, haphazardly deposited debris formed a sturdy barrier that was preventing Will, tucked in his protective haven, from plummeting to his death over the side of the elevated cliff.

"Are ya alright, boy?"

Will stumbled towards him, nodded marginally, and gripped the single feather more tightly in his hand. He started crying, his shoulders were heaving up and down and his body trembled erratically.

The man dismounted and tucked a rough, wool blanket around the sludge-drenched boy. "You're fine. We've found you."

Will looked up at the tall man and noticed the deep channels in the man's cheeks that ran all the way down under the down-turned corners of his mouth, and there were two deep creases on his forehead. Will reckoned a man would have to frown for fifty years straight in a row to get such a grouchy set to his face, but the man's grumpy expression was the most welcome sight he had seen in all his life. He took hold of the big man's calloused hand. The large, gruffly fella gave the boy's hand a firm but tender squeeze in response.

"You must have been terrified," the sullen man spoke gently, "but you're safe now." He helped Will mount up onto the back of the horse and clicked his tongue to get the horse rolling. The horse crooked her ears and quivered her mane, trying to look back, but the man held her firmly by the tether.

As the horse followed her master's lead, Will twisted around and glimpsed behind him—to steal one more look at his star-crossed fawn. Then hot tears gushed down the eight-year-old's cheeks and the mare carried him to safety down the steep, rock-strewn path.

"Pearl," my jaw dropped, "you said that was a heartwarming story and I was going to love it."

She nodded tentatively.

I shook my head. "It wasn't heartwarming. It was the most bizarre, grotesque, sad... disturbing story I've *ever* heard." I drummed my nails on the kitchen table. "And I am a psychologist," I added in order to validate my previous statement. (Although, I didn't deem it necessary to disclose that I hadn't *actually* seen a *real* patient yet.) I addressed the hound dog, "Was that a sweet, heartwarming story, Hank?"

"Nooo." Hank's head wobbled energetically triggering sprays of slobber to splatter sporadically across the kitchen floor.

"See? Even Hank agrees." I stared, with distaste, at my plate. "I can't even finish eating my bologna sandwich now."

"I'll eat it." Will said.

I slid my plate in his direction.

"It was heartwarming," Pearl attempted to explain, "because the angel visited Will."

"Oh, I see." My fingers started drumming on the tabletop again. "Do you think the fact that Will shot a fawn, who was half-eaten up by wild animals, most likely while it was still alive, then the poor thing ended up floating beside him during the time he was hunkered down in a hollowed log surrounded by floodwater, and eventually saved his life

25

when its body lodged at the foot of a cliff thus breaking his fall, doesn't somehow taint the heartwarming essence of this story?"

"Well," Pearl deliberated briefly, "when you put it like that, I guess heartwarming may not be the *perfect* word to summarize his tale. But, on the bright side, Will made it through because his angel helped him." She reached over and squeezed his hand.

"Perhaps," I reflected on Pearl's relentlessly bright-sided nature.

Pearl thoughtfully expounded, "An angel's duties are not solely the praise of God in the heavenly sphere but the actual care of human beings on earth," her head tilted wistfully, "and animals too."

"Will, I bet your family was in a state of panic worrying about you." My hand rose to cover my heart. "I can't even imagine."

"Nooo," Will imitated Hank precisely, "obviously my mama didn't realize what was going on and the big Van Dyke farm was destroyed and the entire family drowned. My uncle and aunt, and cousins, Mary, Gina, Grady, and Josh all died when the water swept through the house." He took a drink of soda before continuing, "The Elkhorn Creek swelled into a roaring torrent. On its crest rode miner's cabins, parts of bridges, and occasionally a body of a woman or child. Many people fled to the hills, but scores were caught in the seething floods and met their death. The town of Keystone was swept out of existence and the flood wiped out a settlement called Shakrege in an hour. Nearly everyone and every living thing in Elkhorn district died. Everything was wiped out, the cattle and horses drowned by the hundreds. At the time it was considered the most dreadful catastrophe in West Virginia's history."

"That's so sad, Will. It must have been the worst day of your life."

"Nah," Will's lips pursed, "I've had worse."

Pearl insightfully interjected, "You see, Annie, sometimes what seems like a person's worst day of their life may actually be their best day."

"That's true. It was a good day for me because I survived and I survived because I had my angel watching over me." He winked at me. "Knowing that you have an angel to guide you through the hard times is a fine feeling. It makes ya think ya have the world by the tail with a downhill pull."

"I've never had an angel visit me," I replied disheartened.

Will informed me, "There are times or seasons when a person needs to have an angel protecting and surrounding them and maybe you haven't needed special protection in your lifetime yet."

"Possibly..."

"Annie, if you ever need an angel to come to your rescue they'll be there."

"All of this may be the *cat's meow*, but I still do not feel that story qualifies as a heartwarming tale."

"Truue," Hank chimed in.

I was still processing what happened during his fateful day and suddenly blurted out, "Did you ever go hunting again?"

Will adjusted his hearing aid. "Did I ever go hunting again?" he repeated my question.

"Yes, did you hunt after the fawn incident?"

"Nah, I never much had the stomach to hunt after that experience, and fortunately I was never put in the position where I needed to slaughter an animal for food." He thoughtfully pondered, "Although, I did have to kill a human being once."

Argonne Forest, France
October 2, 1918
The Lost Battalion
{{4}}

When the Major described them as "The Lost Battalion," Will silently deliberated on the fact that in this case it wasn't really a "battalion" because a battalion is made up of four companies, each with one to two hundred men, and this was actually seven companies of infantry with a machine gun company.

"Why are ya sayin' we're lost, Major?" Will asked. "We know where we are. Don't we?"

"Of course we know where we are," Major Whittlesey looked at Will as if he had a few marbles loose, "but we don't know where our fellow forces are. Do ya understand, soldier? We are lost because we've been abandoned."

"*Abandoned?*" Will gulped. His eyes dropped to the ground and he trudged along beside five hundred and fifty-three other men through the dense Argonne Forest. Their objective, Will knew, had been to reach a place called Charlevaux Road then up to Hill 198. He was exhausted, having fought hard for months, and all he wanted was to go home and see Erma again. He and the other soldiers quietly managed to slip through an unmanned gap in the German positions on Hill 198 when Major Whittlesey ordered his men to move down the road, and take the backside of the hill. Will fell into position, alongside his fellow combatants, and helped set up the machine guns on the flanks to the East and the West. Runner posts, he noticed, were set up every one hundred yards or so along the route, so the battalion could stay in contact with the main military body to the rear. Instead of using radios, they were using human runners, dogs, and even carrier pigeons to send information among command posts.

About an hour later, Roger Ireland, a fellow from New York City, returned from a run and reported that the surrounding terrain was clear of enemy. So Major Whittlesey told them to dig in for the night. The hillside was hard and rocky, so Will dropped down low and began clearing a place to sleep for the night. He lay prone in a "funk" hole that night, shivering from the cold, waiting for the dawn. Since they had moved so quickly off of Charlevaux Road he had left behind his wool blanket and overcoat and he felt like kicking himself for being so lame-brained.

He could hear a brook running along the bottom of the hill and it put him in mind of the creek that ran alongside his home in West Virginia. He had spent many a night falling asleep, with the window half ajar, listening to and being lulled by the burbling stream. *"Oh, how I wish I were home."* He pulled out a beaten journal and a pencil and scribbled a short letter to Erma, all the time hoping he would live long enough to tear the page from the book and mail it, along with a dozen other letters he had written to her—if he made it through the night.

2nd October 1918

Dearest Erma,

The weather has been wet and the ground muddy here in the Argonne Forest. In many ways the forest puts me in mind of the great mountains of West Virginia during the rainy season. The forest is dense, the ground covered with dazzling jade-colored moss, and the trees that are still standing have trunks so wide they must have been here for hundreds of years. If it weren't for the nearly constant sound of guns firing and shells thundering I could close my eyes and imagine I am home.

Tomorrow is my twenty-forth birthday and I feel so thankful to be alive. Every night when I close my eyes I thank God I made it through another day. This makes me appreciate life, even when death looms around every turn in the road. It's kind of ironic that being around so much death and destruction causes me to appreciate my life more than I ever realized. Too many people have died here, and for what?

To tell ya the truth, I'm sad to be fighting the Germans, but when I see how they have ruined so many innocent folk's lives, and you see a poor child lying with his brains blown out by a German bullet, it is hard to have any sympathy for them.

I am hunkered down in my "funk" hole (that's what we call our trenches) and at this moment it is quiet and I can hear the sound of a creek gurgling a few yards away. Things aren't as bad here as they are in some places. I ran into one fella that told me the underfoot in the trenches by the swamp areas were so awful that he put on a new pair of ammunition boots and within no time the heels and soles had rotted off. My boots are still in fine shape and keeping my feet warm. I am grateful for this. Hopefully I can survive and not get the dreaded trench foot.

I miss you and can't wait to see you again. I will write again as soon as I can.

Your dear friend,
Will

At daybreak, on the morning of his birthday, Will fell in line with the others and within less than half an hour of trudging along, the group suddenly comprehended that Germans had surrounded them.

"We're cut off from the rest of the Allied forces," Major Whittlesey shouted. His hand frantically motioned for everyone to take cover. They soon discovered the rear was also closed off. They had no way out. Surrounded, knowing there would be no more ammunition coming and no reinforcements to help, the troops dug in. The Germans sent a near-constant barrage of machine gun fire, mortar shells, sniper fire, and ground attacks led by flamethrowers. The sniper fire, it appeared, was the most life threatening at the moment and Will screamed out in sheer horror when Private George Bigelow took it upon himself to stand and charge in the direction of the assassin.

"What in the tarnation is he doing? Has he lost his mind?"

A return shot had taken Private Bigelow back into a shell hole, where he laid at the bottom, most likely dead.

Will could see that he had taken a series of bullets in the chest and face. He reached out toward the wounded soldier, wondering if he could manage to fumble to the hole beside him. *"It's only a few feet away."*

He surveyed the area outside of his protective trench and figured he may be able to crawl through the mud on his front, if he kept low, and help Private Bigelow. He could see his friend's face frozen in a mask of frightful terror, blood gushing from his mouth and nose when he tried to speak. He could not believe it at all—it did not seem possible to him that Private George Bigelow, with whom he had spent every hour and every day in close companionship for so many months past, was dying.

All around him Will could hear hardened soldiers weeping. He listened to the wounded men who were crying out for help as the sniper's bullets rained down on them. The thick acrid artillery smoke crept in around him, but the injured soldiers were just out of reach because of the deadly German guns. He started praying for the strength to rise up, crawl over and pull the battered men to safety. He rose, retreated, and then rose again trying to capture his courage.

"Don't be afraid." Will heard a regal voice drone through the barrage of shells and sniper fire ringing out.

He looked toward the heavens where a familiar figure soared above him. He briefly wondered if anyone else could see the form. The outline glinted, sparkled; an orb surrounded the angelic form protecting it from the downpour of explosions. Will remembered when he was a child hovering in the hollow of a log in the midst of the great flood. He unexpectedly recalled the angel's visit on that dreadful day with perfect clarity.

"Be still," the angel spoke.

Will stared at him for a long moment before finally murmuring, "Alrighty, then. Thank ya."

Just then an explosion tore across the already beaten landscape and a chorus of artillery lit up. The force of the explosion sent Will rolling down the hill like a greased log. Coming to a rest at the bottom again, he tried to block out the hissing bangs shrieking in the distance. He began to crawl back over the new layer of sludge toward his own "funk" hole but the hill was steep on this side. *I can play dead. I can move inch-by-inch back to safety. I won't let the Germans capture and torture me for information.* He held tight to his weapon as he slowly crept up the hill. The shells became louder and louder on the battlefield.

"Be still," the angel spoke to him again.

Will froze. He dropped his face down into the muck. He

could hear footsteps behind him. He wrapped his finger around the trigger and attempted to calm his breath. *"Don't move."* He lay there for long moments in the brush surrounding him as the footfalls of several men passed on the road just below him. He counted six men but he couldn't be sure. Once he could no longer hear the sound of boots pounding along the rocky road he raised his head and studied the area.

What he saw terrified him. A young man, barely sixteen years old, he estimated, was pointing a rifle at him. The German soldier was standing only a few yards away and Will noticed he was shaking. Will stared at the boy, meeting his eyes, and rolled over completely to face him. The German said something that Will did not understand, but what he did understand was the look the other soldier had in his eyes. *"He's going to kill me."*

Calmly, Will tentatively fell back onto one elbow, aimed, and when the soldier hesitated, he shot the boy straight between his eyes. It all happened in a flash of a second. The boy wasn't expecting it. Will watched the other soldier fall in a heap to the ground. His eyes brimmed with tears that did not fall. A single feather dropped unhurriedly from the sky. He reached up and grabbed the snowy white quill and tucked it into his pocket. Will rolled back over and his angel's protective light was shining down on him as he edged up the hill toward the mortifying thunder. He didn't dare look back.

When he reached the top of the hill all he could see was destruction. The very place where he had dug in for the night, the place where he had left Private Bigelow, and the whole limitless area had been bombed. All that remained was a deep mortar hole.

Several hours later, Will was able to meet up with Major

Whittlesey and the remaining troops some hundred yards from their original position.

"I thought you were dead."

Will stroked the back of his neck while he spoke. "I thought I was too, sir."

"Every runner I've dispatched has either became lost or they've ran into German patrols, so carrier pigeons are the only method of communicating with headquarters," Major Whittlesey told him exasperatedly.

The following morning, the troops understood that inaccurate coordinates were delivered by one of the pigeons and the unit was subjected to friendly fire, so they sent up another pigeon, named Cher Ami, to deliver the following message:

WE ARE ALONG THE ROAD PARALLEL TO 276.4
OUR ARTILLERY IS DROPPING A BARRAGE
DIRECTLY ON US.
FOR HEAVEN'S SAKE!
STOP IT!

Of the five hundred fifty-four men who were on the hill, one hundred seven died and one hundred fifty-nine were wounded.

Will was one of the lucky ones. He made it home, in one piece, and he believed it was because an angel was there to protect him.

Sissonville, West Virginia
September 12, 1981
A Carroty-Colored Dress
{{5}}

I wondered if the letter he referred to was safely tucked in the ornately decorated jewelry chest in the attic. I was aware that Will had written to Erma quite often while he was serving in WWI, because I had found the letters he had sent to her a few months earlier when I was rummaging through the books, chests, crates, and boxes that cluttered the tiny bay on the upper floor.

I also knew Will had been in love with our mutual friend, Erma, for many years, and it was through Erma that he and I became friends. It was that friendship that ultimately spurred me to buy this old farmhouse up Black Hollow Road. Suddenly, I flashed back to a conversation that took place a few months earlier when I was trying to determine whether I should tell Will that I had discovered his letters stored in Erma's attic.

Unexpectedly, I blurted out, "I found a box of letters that you had written to Erma during World War I up in the attic."

"She kept them?" he asked, with a note of surprise in his voice.

"Evidently so," I nudged him, "do you want them back?

"No," he winked, "not right now."

"I won't read them," I promised. "I just opened a box and saw an envelope... it looked like you wrote to her a lot back then."

"I don't mind if ya read them. I was a young kid back then, in love with Erma, very afraid, and reluctantly stationed on the other side of the world. There were folks dying all over the place." He paused to consider before confiding, *"Heck, the very first time I was fired on I peed my britches. What kind of man would pee in his government issued uniform?"*

A long silence preceded my answer, "A scared man?"

He replied gratefully, "I was as scared as a sinner in a cyclone, I can assure you of that."

Obviously I wasn't going to mention the letters stored in the attic to Will again, especially since Pearl was sitting there with us, so I let them chatter for a few minutes. Then when Will and Pearl had finished up the gourmet lunch I had prepared, I lifted their plates, walked over to the sink, plunged my hands back into the dishwater, chased around for the dishcloth, and then energetically scrubbed the nonstick pot I'd used to burn the ravioli.

"There is one other thing I'd like to request," Pearl said rather sheepishly.

"Okay. What do you want?" With a hard jerk, I pulled the stubborn sink plug, slapped it down on the counter, and turned on the water to rinse out the clumps of charred ravioli.

"I was wondering if you'd stand up for me in the wedding. You know, would you consider being my bridesmaid?"

I shifted my weight uncomfortably as I painstakingly thought through her proposal. "What would you want me to wear?"

"Well, I'm wearing a pearl-colored dress."

"Naturally."

"I was thinking that perhaps you could be dressed in orange to match the shade of the foliage in the fall," she added for further clarification, "since the wedding will be held outside."

"Seriously? Orange?" I took into consideration my limited wardrobe choices and quickly ascertained that I did not own one stitch of orange clothing—not even an orange sock. "What shade of orange? Auburn? Ginger?" (You see, when someone asks me to stand up at their wedding I want to make sure I am perfectly clear about what I'm going to be donning.)

"Carroty," Pearl elucidated.

"The color of a carrot?" I asked, trying to visualize this in my mind.

"Yes."

"A peeled carrot or an unpeeled carrot?"

"Peeled." She pointed toward the hound dog. "And since Hank is going to be the best man, so to speak, he'll need a carroty tie to wear."

Hank's head boosted up alertly, *"Huhh?"*

"Shhh," I directed a quick visual warning in his direction as if he were a three-year-old child about to point out the proverbial elephant in the room. *"Geeze, I wonder where I'll find a dress the color of a peeled carrot? How much it will cost? Maybe the Goodwill will have something I can afford."*

"I'm not persnickety," Pearl graciously offered up, "any dress will do as long as it is carroty."

It was crystal clear that I needed to kindly respond. "I would love to be your bridesmaid, and I will start shopping for a new carroty dress tomorrow when I drive into Charleston." I plastered a wide, bright smile across my face.

"Thank you." Pearl beamed. "I want to purchase the

dress for you so, if you'd like, we can go to the Diamond Department Store and peruse the selection in the ladies' fine apparel department together."

"Okay, that sounds fine, but you don't need to buy my dress."

"I insist." Pearl pursed her lips in determination.

I glanced down to notice Tessy tugging on Hank's ear again. *"Quitt!"* The ole hound dog pleaded pathetically before releasing a very loud and extended spurt of intestinal gas. I considered all the treats Will had been giving him, and presumed it was healthy for the ole dog— although not so pleasant for those of us positioned within the six-foot radius surrounding him.

Pearl took off her thick brown glasses and then spent a long time wiping the frames with the hem of her skirt before raising the edge to cover her nostrils, in a not so subtle attempt to block the wafting reek perpetrating around us.

Tessy, smelling the newly released puff of poof mingled with the not so fragrant scent of burnt ravioli, ran—at break neck speed—to the living room to seek refuge underneath the buffer provided by the overstuffed, albeit hair-encrusted, living room couch.

Will started laughing, coughed a couple of times (or perhaps he was gagging, I wasn't quite sure), and then suggested, "Let me tell ya'll a joke." He grinned exultantly. "The elderly widow who lives next door to me went to the doctor complaining of 'silent gas.' She'd been passing silent gas a lot lately, including several times since she had been in the doctor's office. The doctor broke the news to her, 'The first thing we need to do is get you a hearing aid.' "

Pearl started cackling hysterically and lowered the hem of her dress from her nose. Her high-pitched laughter was infectious, and she had a wonderful, lazy way of grinning that made me want to smile. She abruptly rose and carried her glass to the sink. "Are ya ready, Will?"

"No, I want to talk to Annie for a spell but I'll walk ya to your car."

"Okay." Pearl turned to me and posed, "Annie, are you going to pick me up in the morning?"

"Yes, indeed."

"Alrighty then, I'll see you in the morning."

I escorted my friends to the front door and just as they were walking out Will turned to me and whispered, "Annie, I don't bring groceries up here because I think you can't afford them, I bring 'em up 'cause you're 'bout the worst cook I've ever met."

I forcibly smacked the screen door shut behind him and could still hear him chuckling as he ambled across the front porch, down the short path, and opened the door of Pearl's car. I saw him give her a peck on the cheek.

I stepped out and waited on the front porch and when he returned we parked ourselves on the comfy couch.

"Let me tell ya a story, Annie."

"Is it heartwarming?" I wondered, though didn't dare ask.

Charleston, West Virginia
March 15, 1930
Forewarning
{{6}}

The frosty, frigid mists that passed for winter rains hung over Charleston and for days on end the sun refused to shine. The browns stayed brown and the bare limbs stayed stark. The chilly days and the soggy winds of the night continued throughout February and into the Ides of March. Will and his coworker, Theo, hovered behind the protective limestone wall of the East Wing and opened their lunch boxes.

"What did Lillian fix ya for lunch today, Will?" Theo asked.

Will removed the wax paper from his sandwich and peeked in between the two slices of bread. "It looks like a meatloaf sandwich," he explored the contents of his metal box a little further, "and a paper bag full of Bit-O-Honey bars."

"Your wife packs a good lunch."

"Yep. I have a sweet tooth so she always packs me something sugary." He opened the paper bag and offered a Bit-O-Honey bar to Theo, "Have you tasted one of these yet?"

"No. I can't say that I have." Theo accepted the bag from Will and withdrew a large bar of the wrapped jiff. He removed the waxed paper and outer wrapping before popping a segment into his mouth. He washed it down with a gulp of coffee straight from his thermos. "These are tasty, thanks."

"You're welcome."

"Hey Will," Theo broached, "my brother-in-law just took on a job, down around Gauley Bridge, digging a tunnel. I think he called it a hydroelectric project. He said they were going to be paying twenty cents an hour more than we're earning now, so I'm thinking about heading down there and seeing if I can get hired-on."

"Twenty cents more per hour?" Will repeated. "That adds up quickly."

"Yeah," Theo agreed, "and as I'm sure you've noticed, since the temporary 'Pasteboard Capitol' burned down a couple weeks ago they've been pushin' us a little hard here. Don't ya think?"

"They can push us all they want but we can't set the limestone any faster than we are." Will glanced around at the partially completed Supreme Court Chambers where they were squatting down behind a marble column trying to escape the cold wind. "Plus, they are gonna be constructing this building for at least five more years, so it's a good job." He shrugged, "I feel a certain pride being able to tell folks that I'm building the new state capitol. It's gonna be a piece of history that will be here forever."

"Maybe," Theo said, "but I'm going to go down and check it out. You should come with me."

Will knew that Lillian wouldn't be too keen on moving away from her family. "I doubt my wife will want to move."

"I'm not going to move down there," Theo explained, "I'll be bunking with a few fellas while I'm working then I'll come home a couple days every week to visit the family. You could do the same thing."

"Twenty cents an hour," Will cyphered for a flash, "would be 'bout eight dollars a week."

"Yeah, it's good money. You think it over and talk to Lillian about it. I'm sure you could bunk with the rest of us

---

42

if you decided to go."

"It's something to consider. I'll talk to Lillian tonight and let ya know tomorrow," Will ensured.

"Sounds fine," Theo tucked his thermos back into his lunch box. "Hey, Will, could I have a couple of those Bit-O-Honey bars to take home to the kids?"

"Sure," Will handed him the bag, "take 'em all."

Later that evening, Lillian dolloped another heaping portion of chowder into Will's bowl.

"This is some mighty fine chowder, Lillian. Ya added some peas to it tonight, didn't ya?"

"Yes, I did. I'm glad ya like it." Lillian's face beamed at his compliment.

That's when he decided to explain Theo's plan to his wife. "A fella at work, Theo, was tellin' me today that he's gonna try to get a job down around Gauley Bridge. They're building a tunnel at Hawks Nest and they're gonna be hiring a lot of men for the job. He said they were paying twenty cents more per hour than we are earning working on the state capitol."

Lillian gently placed her spoon on the table. "Will, I don't want to move. I love living here on the East Side."

"I know this is a fine apartment, and you wouldn't have to move. Theo is planning to bunk up with his brother-in-law and some other men while they're working during the week and come home for the weekends."

Lillian seemed to contemplate this cautiously. "I reckon eight dollars a week might well be worth the inconvenience of you having to travel back and forth between Gauley

Bridge and Charleston."

Will was surprised at her response.

She continued, "But this is a decision you will have to make and I'll support whatever you decide."

By the time he settled into their warm feather bed Will had decided he would go down to Gauley Bridge with Theo and apply for a position building the Hawks Nest Tunnel.

Around two o'clock in the morning, Will thought he heard a familiar voice say, "Don't be afraid!" He opened his eyes and saw a blazing light floating above him. The mystical figure was his guardian angel. Will closed his eyes and decided he must be dreaming.

"Be still," the voice told him.

Goose bumps trickled throughout his entire body. His eyes shot open again and he looked over at Lillian. She was still sleeping. The voice had not awakened her. He knew the voice, and he was not afraid of it; the voice loved Will. The voice was there to help him.

"Am I dreaming?" he asked aloud.

"Be still," the thundering vision demanded.

Will wondered why Lillian wasn't hearing the voice, because it was as loud as any physical voice he had ever heard.

"What do you want me to know?" he whispered.

"Be still."

"I don't understand," Will replied apologetically.

"The tunnel is not safe."

Will knew right then that the warning was a premonition—a forewarning. He would be still. He would stay put. He would not accompany Theo on his trip to Gauley Bridge. He would not seek out a job building the Hawks Nest Tunnel. His eyes fluttered for a moment then he effortlessly drifted back into a deep and peaceful sleep.

—

Will later learned that the Hawks Nest Tunnel ended up being one of the worst industrial disasters in American history. When workers found the mineral silica in the mountain they began to mine it. The workers were given no masks or breathing equipment and ended up developing silicosis, which is a respiratory disease. Most of the workers died from silicosis within a year—including Theo. While there is not a definite number of how many people died of silicosis, a Congressional hearing later placed the death toll at between five hundred and three thousand workers, and Will believed that his angel had most likely saved his life—once again.

Sissonville, West Virginia
September 13, 1981
Sweet Treats
{{7}}

All the next morning I kept rolling over the idea of angels appearing to us in our dreams, and was still rolling the notion over in my mind when I noticed it was time to go pick up Pearl.

"Hank, you can't go with me this morning," I apologetically informed my friend.

"Nooo."

"I can't have you wait in the car for me while Pearl and I go shopping at the Diamond Department Store."

"Nooo," he pleaded pitifully.

"I need you to stay here and take care of Tessy," I explained as I cracked the door open.

He attempted to escape. "No, Hank! I mean it."

"Saaad," he whined.

"I know it makes you sad. It makes me feel sad too. But, please do it for me." I rubbed his jaw with my hand—all the time knowing it would be covered with smarmy slobbers—then swiped it across the leg of my Lee jeans. I squeezed out the barely cracked door, locked it, jumped into my Volkswagen convertible, turned the radio on, and cranked up the volume.

Super Duper Charlie Cooper, the DJ on the radio, was playing "Another Brick in the Wall" by Pink Floyd when I pulled into Pearl's driveway. She was waiting for me on the front porch and quickly hopped into the passenger's seat.

"I love Pink Floyd, don't you?" Pearl asked.

"Yes, I do." I peeked at her curiously. "Tell me, how is it

that you are familiar with Pink Floyd?"

"I may be old, but I am still a hippy-chick. I keep up with rock 'n roll trends." She teasingly rolled her eyes. "Could you turn it up a notch?"

"Sure." I twisted the knob on the radio.

We sang along with our heads bobbing to the beat as we passed Dawson's farm, followed the road running beside Pocatalico River and eventually passed Sissonville Middle School and the Sissonville Sheriff's Headquarters. I drew her attention to the sheriff's office as we whizzed by. "Sheriff Holmes doesn't seem to care much for me," I told Pearl. I turned the volume on the radio down a notch so she could hear me.

"Why's that?"

"I'm not sure." I shrugged. "When I told him that I suspected Buster Thaxton wasn't a criminal but perhaps had a mental illness he regarded me with abundant disfavor—the negative waves weren't too difficult to pick up on."

"He can be a bit..." Pearl seemed to deliberate on the best word to convey, "stern," she finally posed, "but he sure does love Hank."

"True."

"What happened between you and Buster anyway?"

My thoughts floated back to a spring day in April.

I found a tattered crate and carried it over to the walnut tree where I started dropping shells and fallen limbs, left from the winter storms, into the wooden box to later throw out behind the barn. I was humming "The Rose" by Bette Midler, when I heard footsteps lumbering noisily through the thick brush. I turned around, expecting to see that Hank finally woke up from his sixth nap of the day, but instead I witnessed a man who froze and stared sharply in my direction.

"Can I help you?" I asked, as my heartbeat quickened and my gut twisted into a tight ball.

He didn't look me straight in the eyes, nor did he answer, as he kept striding blunderingly in my direction. I dropped the crate to the ground and ran in a full state of panic toward the house.

I heard Hank growl, deep from within his throat, before barking out a piercing warning. He took off running toward the unknown man and loyally positioned his large body between us. The man started kicking his leg wildly in the dog's direction. Hank leapt onto his shoulders, forcefully knocking the intruder down into the mud. The man kept trying to strike Hank until the old dog expertly situated his mouth around the man's throat. I threw open the screen door, slammed the wooden door shut, and immediately dialed the sheriff's office. "This is Annie," I managed to sputter, "I am located on Erma's farm up Black Hollow Road and there is an unknown man on the property." I peeked out the window, "Hank has him pinned on the ground, and I need help!"

"Did you say Black Hollow Road?"

"Yes," I panted, and stared at the front door.

"Not to worry," the dispatcher responded. "Sheriff Holmes is out your way, I'll give him a call right now. Don't hang up. Stay on the line with me, honey."

Within less than three minutes, which felt like thirty, I heard the sheriff's car speeding up the hollow with the siren blasting. His cruiser slid as he shoved on the breaks, tossing gravel into the air. He jumped from his vehicle, withdrew a pistol, and ran over to where Hank was standing resolutely on top of the man. "Good job,

Hank." I could overhear the sheriff saying, "Ya can let go of his throat now. I have this covered." Hank released his gripped teeth before his gaze raised toward Sheriff Holmes. The hound dog glanced down at the man one more time, and viciously snarled, before stepping off his chest.

"The dog tried to kill me!" The man bawled as his shaking hands rose to cover his throat. "I hate dogs!" He clenched his fists, "I'm scared of 'em."

"Oh heck, it looks to me like he didn't even break your skin." The sheriff looked at him long and hard. "Well, I'll be," Sheriff Holmes boomed as he spit into the dirt, "if it ain't Buster Thaxton. We've been looking for you for over two months now." He motioned for the man to roll over as he withdrew a pair of handcuffs from his belt and shackled them around the man's wrists. "What in the tarnation are you doin' all the way up here?" He nudged the man with his boot. "Get up, Buster. You're gonna get a first-class, chauffeured ride to the station." The sheriff escorted Buster to the back of his car, placed his hand on top of his head and shoved him into the back seat before slamming the door shut. He walked to the front door of the farmhouse and rapped twice. When I unbolted the door, he could easily ascertain the terror masked on my face.

"Are you alright, Ma'am?"

I nodded numbly.

"He didn't hurt ya, did he?"

I trembled, "No." I gulped back the lump that was forming in my throat, "Hank stopped him."

"Hank is a fine fellow," the sheriff acknowledged as he glanced down at the dog who was now seated proudly beside the officer. "You are lucky Hank was here, 'cause

Buster Thaxton is a mean man—a wanted criminal. It's hard to tell what could have happened if Hank hadn't been here to protect ya."

"Well, thank you Sheriff," I sighed, "for getting up here so quickly."

"You're welcome, Ma'am." He tipped his ball cap. "Is there anyone you can call to come up and stay with ya for a bit 'til ya calm down?"

"Yes, I'll call Will. He'll come up here and stay with me."

"Will?" The sheriff grinned from ear to ear, "How's Will doing? I know he was mighty upset after Erma passed away."

"He's doing fine, I suppose."

"Good. Tell him Sheriff Holmes sends his regards."

"What happened between me and Buster?" I repeated Pearl's question. "Well, after Erma passed on over to the sweet by and by, and before I decided to buy Erma's farmhouse, I was cleaning up the yard one day and Buster suddenly appeared from nowhere. He scared me, Hank jumped on top of him, and I telephoned Sheriff Holmes."

"Oh." Pearl wrung her hands. "What did Sheriff Holmes do?"

"He arrested him." I glanced in her direction. "He said Buster was a wanted criminal."

She sighed. "Did you know I've requested to be Buster's caregiver?"

"Yes, Will mentioned it."

"I think since my son was autistic I'll be able to help Buster," Pearl provided an unsolicited explanation.

"You're an angel."

Pearl clicked her tongue. "I may be on the same side of

the angels but I can assure you that I'm not one."

I giggled.

A comfortable silence encircled us as I turned onto the I-77 ramp leading toward Charleston.

Pearl curiously asked, "Do you have a favorite saint?"

"A favorite saint?" I repeated. Thinking it through for a moment I finally answered, "My talents include multitasking, listening to other people's problems, and taking in strays. Basically, I'm a sucker for just about any lost cause. So, I guess I would choose Saint Jude, the patron saint of hope and impossible causes."

"What about Saint Francis of Assisi, the lover of all creatures and protector of animals?"

"Yeah," I bobbed my head, "he's a good saint, too. Saint Francis was a male, right?"

"I think so," Pearl sighed, "my favorite saint is Saint Christopher because he is the patron saint of travelers and of children. Since my son was autistic, I've sent many prayers up asking for him to watch over my boy when he was still alive."

"I'm sure it was difficult at times."

"It was worth it," she assured.

"How is it you know all the saints, Pearl? I wasn't aware The United Methodist Church taught a whole lot about saints."

Pearl sighed, "I almost married a Catholic man many years ago. He knew all the saints and the history of each one of them. It nearly broke my mama's heart when I dated outside of our religion, and ultimately she forbade me to continue seeing the young man." She shrugged her shoulders. "It all worked out in the end."

I had no idea how to respond so I diverted the conversation. "Hey, did you know that Erma and her friend

Ida worked at the Diamond Department Store?"

"Will mentioned something about Erma working there, but I wasn't aware that her friend Ida worked there too."

"Yes, they worked there from the time they left Thurmond in 1915 and continued to work for Mr. Geary until around 1925, I believe."

"I know you were friends with Erma but did you know Ida too?"

"She was my college professor and very good friend. As a matter of fact, Ida introduced me to Erma."

"Will told me they were good friends."

"The best," I verified.

I made a sharp turn onto Capitol Street and slowed my speed. Pearl rolled down her window. "Can you smell The Peanut Shoppe?" She took in a deep satisfying breath.

"Mmm, hmm." I tapped on the breaks to slow our path. "Do you want to stop?"

"If you don't mind. I rarely get into Charleston."

"Not a problem."

I pulled alongside the Kanawha County Public Library and parked the car. Pearl was giddy. She jabbered excitedly as we walked down the street. "Did you know The Peanut Shoppe opened back in the 1950s and has had a booming business ever since."

"I can smell why." The aroma of hot roasted cashews and Spanish nuts wafting out the door caused my mouth to water in anticipation.

"Yes, and some of their recipes for the confections date back to the early 1920s."

"Wow," I opened the door and allowed her to enter in front of me.

"Look," Pearl pointed towards the nuts toasting in their shell on an antique planter's gas-burning roaster. She was literally like a kid in a candy store. I enjoyed watching her excitement as she carefully selected which items to buy. Caramels, pulled creams, and hot roasted cashews were ultimately chosen, and I settled on a bag of Spanish nuts.

We walked back to my Volkswagen, stashed our treats in the backseat and headed toward the Diamond Department Store to find a carroty dress.

"Will's a pig when it comes to sweets so don't tell him I bought these goodies," Pearl requested.

"What goodies?" I gave her a wink.

Later that afternoon, when I reached the top of the mountain up Black Hollow Road, I could see Will, Hank and Tessy seated on the front porch of my newly acquired farmhouse.

"How'd ya'll make out?" Will asked, "Did you and Pearl find ya a carroty dress?"

"We made out just fine. I am the proud owner of a new flowing crepe, carroty dress." My nose scrunched up. "But to tell you the truth, Will, the dress makes me look more like a pumpkin than a carrot."

He chuckled. "Annie, you don't weigh no more than a hundred pounds soaking wet, so it's a little hard for me to believe ya'd look like a pumpkin in anything."

"I do." I dropped down on the old couch beside him. "Actually, I have a gold bangle belt to wrap around my waist, so perhaps I can play around with it and look more like a gourd than a pumpkin."

"A gourd?" Will repeated, crossing his arms in front of his chest. "That sounds like a good plan, Annie," he paused transitorily, "I don't know that much 'bout women's stuff like dresses and all." Will shrugged apologetically. "I just came up here to mow the grass."

"I can see that. Thank you."

"No problem."

I tugged my bag of Spanish nuts out and offered him some.

"Did you and Pearl stop by The Peanut Shoppe while ya were in town?" Will inquired.

"Yes," I sheepishly replied.

"Did Pearl buy any goodies?" he asked, swiping a handful of nuts.

"I can't quite recall."

"Humph!" he snorted. "I've been sitting here thinking... and I have a story I wanna share with ya."

"Is it disturbing? You know, like the story about the poor fawn?"

"Nah," he popped a nut into his mouth, "it's heartwarming."

"Heartwarming? Oh no!"

Will stood sporting a two-tone bold panel striped sweater and trim-cut Ivy cuffed slacks outside the car dealership where he had been working for over a year now, slid a chew of Mail Pouch tobacco into his jaw and searched for something to use as a spittoon. He studied his watch and realized he could clock out in ten minutes. It didn't matter that he hadn't sold a car today because he no longer cared. He had enough money.

He disliked this job and felt like a fraud every time he sold an unreliable automobile to one of the trusting folks who worked hard to earn a living. All he wanted to do was go home, see his wife Lillian, get a pint of misty tasting moonshine, and lose himself in *The Spy Who Came in from the Cold.* He halfway considered just hopping into his truck, crossing the bridge before rush hour started, and never looking back. "Nah, I can't do that to Roger," he mumbled under his breath, "at least I should tell him I'm quitting."

Will opened the wide glass door and stepped into the display area. "Roger," he yelled out at the owner seated in a backroom, "I'm going home and I'm not quite sure I'll be back tomorrow."

The man rushed out from his office. "What do you mean? You told me you'd work through the holidays."

Will's brow knit with concentration. "I know I did, Roger. But, I'm getting old, I don't need the money, and some of the jalopies you have on this lot are as worthless as a tit on

55

a boar hog."

"Stay. Please stay. There's nobody who can sell a car like you can," the owner pleaded, "you promised." His head tilted sincerely. "Just work through Christmas Eve. Please don't leave me shorthanded."

Will regarded his wristwatch. *"Five minutes 'til five o'clock."* He started walking down Sixth Street toward the free parking area alongside the riverbank that was maintained as a courtesy of downtown businesses. "I'll sleep on it," he yelled back over his shoulder.

Just as Will opened his truck door, he heard a loud gunshot-like noise and directed his attention toward where the sound had originated. *"The Silver Bridge."* Will saw it was packed full of rush-hour traffic. *"Please, God. No!"* In less than twenty-seconds the entire bridge started folding like a deck of cards. The scene he was witnessing was implausible, too alarming to process in his mind. His eyes fixed on the large structure watching it bending and twisting unnaturally and wondered if this was a figment of his imagination or if, perhaps, he was experiencing a full-blown hallucination.

He heard a familiar, majestic voice boom down from the heavens. "Don't be afraid!" The sound jolted him out of his muddled state of confusion. A white feather drifted tranquilly down in front of him and he didn't even look up—he knew who was addressing him. He plucked the feather out of thin air and tucked it into his trouser pocket. Shouting over his shoulder, "Alrighty then, thank ya," he started running, as fast as his old body would take him, toward the catastrophe. He scurried up the ramp, and yanked open the first car door he came to, "Get out! The bridge is collapsing!"

A young lady popped her gearshift into "Reverse" and

started haphazardly backing down the entrance ramp at full speed. He leapt out of her way, recovered his balance and sprinted to an older-model red Mercury station wagon, tugged open the back door, where three small children were seated, and screamed at the top of his lungs, "Get out of the car!" his voice had more than an edge of urgency. He pulled the youngest child from the vehicle and secured her in his arms.

"What are you doing?" the woman in the front seat screeched in horror.

"The bridge is falling! You have to get off this bridge before your car falls into the river."

The woman scanned her surroundings and a puzzled expression plastered across her face. She saw folks running past her—screams echoed around her. She quickly slid out the driver's side door and scurried to the back seat where she pulled the oldest boy out by his arm and bent in to tug at the hysterical child who had been seated in the middle but was now attempting to climb into the front seat.

"Let's go!" Will directed her.

She followed behind him, holding one child on her hips and dragging the other along by his hand. Will occasionally stopped for a second to pound on a window, all the time attempting to warn the unknowing passengers of the impeding danger. Several panicked motorists followed behind Will as he carried the small child to safety.

The Silver Bridge was fracturing piece-by-piece, section-by-section, as cars plummeted one-by-one into the Ohio River. Will could feel the vibrations of the splintering steel rupturing behind him with each step he took. *I don't think I'll make it.* He shoved the young girl into a hulking man's arms as the floor of the bridge cracked underneath his right foot. "Take her. Take her to safety."

Will stumbled when the bridge fractured underfoot. His right leg plunged into a hole and as he attempted to pull it out a section of tangled steel fell onto his ankle. He shrieked in agony. The beam continued tumbling, chaotically down into the rushing river below. Will rose up onto his elbows and inched his way, dragging his broken leg behind him, toward the ramp of the bridge.

When he looked back he could see the deck bend sharply to the North, spilling its contents into the river, then groaning, it went down in slow-motion on top of the sinking vehicles, crushing many of them against the river bottom. Chaos loomed everywhere. Within seconds all that was visible were dozens of vehicles and wide steel joists littering the cold, mucky river. Will saw a lone tractor-trailer slowly floating down the river, and a man hanging onto a box drifting alongside a heap of rubble.

He could see, standing on Sixth Street, the woman and children he had rescued. Passionate tears were streaming down her cheeks as she held her children close to her chest.

"A dance with death always makes us appreciate life," Will briefly reflected. He plucked the white feather from his pocket and devoted a quick wave to the heavens, "Thank ya," he whispered before all consciousness left him.

Will learned, while lying in the hospital bed with a broken leg and a fractured pelvis, that when the suspended portion of the Silver Bridge collapsed into the river, it took with it thirty-two vehicles, and forty-six victims, including two whose bodies were never found, and he once again thanked God for divine intervention.

Sissonville, West Virginia
September 13, 1981
Good Intentions
{{9}}

"So, you were a hero?"

"I wouldn't exactly say I was a hero," Will beamed at me with unambiguous affection, "and my leg was never the same. I had to start using a walking stick after that."

"You saved those children and helped others get off the bridge before they fell to their death," I placed my hand on his arm, "you were definitely a hero, Will."

"Maybe," he conceded. "All I know is the entire time that I lived in Point Pleasant there was a creature lurking around and it used to give me the heebie-jeebies every time it was mentioned. I kept wondering what I would do if the Mothman visited me."

"The Mothman?"

"Yep. In November of 1966 five men were digging a grave at a cemetery around Clendenin, and they claimed to see a manlike figure flying over the trees. A few days later two young couples from Point Pleasant told the police they saw a large white creature with glowing red eyes while they were driving down a back road. They described it as a large flying man with wings that were almost ten-foot wide."

"I don't know that I want to hang out with you anymore, Will," I gravely informed him, "the weirdest things happen when you are around."

He chuckled before continuing, "Well, during the next few months, other people reported similar sightings. Some folks suggested it was a Sandhill crane, because Sandhill cranes are almost as tall as a man and have a wide wingspan with reddish coloring around the eyes. However, everyone who saw the Mothman said it wasn't a crane. All kinds of people saw him and dreamed 'bout him. Anyway, after the bridge collapsed the Mothman was never sighted again." He shrugged. "I have no idea if the two were connected but most folks figure they were."

"How so?"

"Folks figured the Mothman was like a prophet sending warnings to the residents 'bout the impending bridge collapse. In the end, the two became connected and the Mothman Prophecies are still a legend."

"Wow." I scrunched my nose up. "You're kidding me aren't you?"

"Nah, I wouldn't kid 'bout a thing like the Mothman."

"Weird."

"Yep. The entire incident was very odd. I ended up moving away from Point Pleasant a few months after the bridge collapsed. It was heartbreaking watching the folks trying to deal with the loss of their friends and loved ones, and everywhere I went people would ask 'bout what happened on the bridge, and they wanted me to tell them the story of how I managed to get those children off the bridge in time." He turned to face me, "To tell ya the truth, Annie, I didn't set out to be a hero. It just transpired that way."

"Yeah, I bet most people don't plan on being heroes they just do what they need to do when a problem presents itself."

We gazed out over the yellow-green meadow to the rounded shoulder of the hill.

"Let me ask you something, Will. Do you think I should try to take this old couch to the dump before the wedding ceremony?"

He patted the seat between us. "Definitely not. Why would you do that? This is a fine old couch for a front porch."

"My point exactly. Should one have a couch perched on their front porch? Don't you think it looks... looks... I don't know... odd?"

"Nah. Not up here in the country."

"I'm not trying to put on airs, but wealthy people with nice houses do not have decaying checkerboard couches featured on their front porch."

"Some do," Will assured, "take me for example. I have plenty enough money and I have a couch on my front porch. It's not as fancy as this one, mind ya, but it suits me fine. It's a mighty comfortable seat when I want to relax outside. I've spent heaps of money in my time, but the old couch on my front porch was well worth the ten dollars I paid for it at a yard sale."

"How did you spend most of your money?"

"Some I spent on liquor, some on women, and the rest I spent foolishly."

Will started to laugh so hard he could hardly catch his breath.

I giggled along, truly appreciating his sharp sense of humor.

The following morning, while I was brewing my first pot of coffee for the day, I heard someone pounding on the door. I glanced down at Hank and he peered up at me. He was obviously not concerned over whoever was thumping rhythmically against the wooden entrance. *"He must know*

who is out there." I darted from the kitchen toward the living room. I could see Pearl peeking through the rectangular glass blocks of the door, so I slung it open wide for her to enter.

"Good morning, Pearl. Would you care for a cup of coffee?"

"Thank you." She followed me through the hallway.

I motioned to the kitchen table and she dropped down on a chair, stretched out her legs, and yawned sleepily.

"Black or with cream?"

"Cream please."

While the coffee was slowly dripping into the carafe, I filled Hank and Tessy's bowls up with dry food from a bag. Hank's sad eyes examined it and his head dropped down to the floor. Tessy crawled over the top of Hank's head and began chomping away at the tidbits.

"Annie, did you tell Will we stopped at The Peanut Shoppe?"

"No." I reconsidered. "Okay, yes. However, I didn't tell him you bought anything. Why?"

Pearl's right brow arched inquisitively, "What exactly did you say?"

I searched my memory carefully. "I offered him some Spanish nuts then when he asked me if you bought anything I said I couldn't recall."

"Couldn't recall? Annie, telling him you couldn't recall was like saying, 'Yes, she bought a boat load of delicious, sugary sweet treats.' "

"I'm sorry Pearl. What happened?"

"He ate every one of the pulled creams I had hid in the dishwasher."

"Hid in the dishwasher?"

As if she could read the confusion on my face, she

elaborated, "I don't use my dishwasher as a dishwasher because it's too difficult to hook up and I'd rather just wash the dishes by hand. So, I store my Little Debbie cakes and other special treats in it."

"Oh." I bowed my head like I understood. "I'm so sorry, Pearl. I panicked when he asked me. I didn't want to lie so I avoided answering him. I'll drive you back into Charleston next week and we can pick up anything else you need for the wedding ceremony and stop by The Peanut Shoppe again."

"Maybe..." she drummed her fingers on the tabletop. "I swear, Annie, he'll eat anything that don't eat him first."

"I know Pearl. Will and I have been through a lot together in the last several months and even though he may be a candy hog I can assure you he is a fine man."

"Well, he better keep his sticky fingers out of my dishwasher."

I poured her a cup of coffee, making sure I left room enough for the cream, and slid it across the table along with a can of powdered Coffee-Mate and a spoon. "I was thinking, Pearl. If you are going to ask Buster to the wedding we are going to need to reintroduce him to Hank."

When Hank heard Buster's name his ears perked up with interest. A low growl escaped from deep within his throat and his eyes started darting around the kitchen.

"See," I pointed to the ole hound dog, "just saying his name out loud gets Hank riled up."

"That is a very good idea. Let's pick a day next week and see what we can arrange."

I took a long, satisfying drink of aromatic black coffee.

"Have you talked to that young veterinarian fellow lately? You should invite him to the wedding."

"His name is Bob and I talk to him about every evening

on the telephone, but he's teaching a class this semester in New York, which is why I haven't seen him in four and a half weeks. It's the last class he needs to teach in order to satisfy his scholarship requirements. I mentioned the wedding to him and he said he would see what he could arrange."

"Good. He seems like a fine young man and we could use a veterinarian in this area since Erma passed away. Do you plan to marry him?"

My jaw dropped open in disbelief. "I just met him, Pearl!"

"So? Will and I have only been hoopin' and hollerin' around for a short while and we're tying the knot." She aimed her finger at me. "Before you marry him though, you best make sure he isn't a candy hog like that old ornery fellow I'm going to wed."

"Good point." I nodded in agreement. "I'm not quite sure I am ready to commit to sharing my Little Debbie cakes with anyone just yet."

"Oh," Pearl shrugged her shoulders, "you have to take into consideration which type of cake is your favorite and which type is his favorite. For example, I like Swiss Rolls and Will's favorite is Banana Twins, so we get along just fine. Plus, I'll tell you a little secret but you can't tell Will."

"Okay."

"Promise?"

"Scouts honor." To demonstrate my sincerity, three fingers shot up on my right hand displaying the universal Girl Scout honor salute.

"When we were at The Peanut Shoppe I bought the pulled creams for Will because I knew they were his favorite. I didn't tell him because I enjoy getting his goat, which is why I hid them in the dishwasher, knowing he'd most likely sniff them out. Furthermore," she informed me, "he wouldn't dare eat one of my Little Debbie Swiss Rolls."

I provided a doubtful, albeit honest, look.

"You're right." Her eyes widened. "I'd best be getting home. I need to find a better hiding place."

Suddenly we heard the sound of dry leaves rustling loudly through the open window. The noise sounded as if it was coming from underneath the barn.

"I bet it's the mother cat and kitten I saw out here the other day."

We rushed out the kitchen door toward the barn. Hank followed closely by my side. When we slowed our pace, Hank slowed down too. We paused, and turned up our ears to listen. Hank's head turned in a comical way, as if he too, had pinned his ears back.

"Sounds like they're behind the barn." I motioned for Pearl and Hank to follow me.

The three of us tiptoed around the side of the dilapidated building and peered around the corner. Large drooping clusters of elderberry were leaning against the wooden wall. The large shrubs stood almost twenty feet tall and the black and glaucous blue berries hung plentiful from the vines.

The first face poked out among the sinking bundles. It clearly wasn't a cat. It was knee-height. Then there was another. Pearl suddenly went almost silly with merriment. She reached over and grabbed my arm and pulled me down to the opening to show me the intruders.

The faces were looking up at us. They had comical black masks over their eyes, and busy little black noses. Then one of the raccoons rose on its hind legs, reached up with little hands and grasped a berry straight from the shrub, popped it into its mouth, slurped the juice for quite a long moment, and then swallowed. It then stretched up, selected another elderberry and handed it over to the smaller raccoon hovering curiously behind it.

"Aren't they adorable?" Pearl whispered.

"Nooo," Hank replied, adding a roll of his eyes.

The largest raccoon seemed to smirk at the old dog.

"They're cute," I halfheartedly conceded, "but I'm terrified of raccoons."

"'Coons are nothing to be afraid of, Annie." Pearl curiously investigated the large back yard. "I had no idea Erma had so many elderberries planted. They make great jelly."

"I won't be making any elderberry jelly this year," I promised.

"I understand." She shrugged her shoulders. "Well, I best be movin' on. I need to find a new hiding place for my Little Debbie's before Will comes home." She started walking around the side of the house toward her car. Before the car door thumped shut I heard her yell out, "Don't tell Will that I'm hiding the cakes in a new place!"

"I won't say a word."

After I heard Pearl's car rumble down the rutted hollow, I decided to try putting Hank on a leash. I had seen a leash in Erma's clinic, and thought this might be the best way to train Hank to stay put when we reintroduced him to Buster Thaxton.

"Come on, Hank," I snapped my fingers in his direction, "we're going to try something new."

The old dog reluctantly followed me into the kitchen, down the hallway, and into Erma's clinic. He eyed me suspiciously when I tugged the leash from the hook on the wall.

"Okay, Hank." I took in a deep breath. "We are going to practice using a leash. I am going to hook this end to your collar." I showed him specifically which end I would be using. "Then I'll hold tight to the other end and this way we will always be within a few feet of one another."

"Nooo," Hank peevishly asserted.

"I realize this is not ideal but you are going to have to meet Buster and you can't jump on top of him, knock him to the ground, or clutch his throat with your teeth, because he is a friend of Pearl's and will be visiting the farm from time to time."

"Huhh?"

"Do you understand what I just told you?"

"Yeahh," he wailed.

"Okay, let's try it," I proposed, in an overly upbeat tone of voice.

"Nooo," was once again his response.

The moment I secured the leash hook on his collar—*snap*—he bolted toward the front of the house dragging me through the hallway and into the living room.

"Stop!" I insisted. "Please," I begged.

The hound dog paid no mind as he propelled through the screen door tugging me in his wake. As soon as I heard the wood frame fracture I knew I had made a big mistake. Right before I landed face down on the front porch I must have released my grip on his collar because when my head lifted up I could see Will standing there cackling like an old hen, with Hank by his side.

Will slid his Mail Pouch from the front pocket of his overalls. "Is everything goin' alright 'round here?"

I embarrassedly stood, swiped the dirt from my shirt, and informed him sarcastically, "Just peachy."

"Why didn't ya just let loose of the leash? Hank is nearly twice your size, ya know?"

"In my defense," I puffed up, "I am trying to train Hank

so that he will not attack Buster when Pearl brings him up here."

"Ya don't need a leash, Annie, a good ole Kumbaya will work."

"Kumbaya?" My face distorted questioningly.

"Yep," he slid a smidgen of tobacco in his jaw, "we'll all get together, share some jerky, hug a little bit, and everything will be just fine."

"Seriously?"

He nonchalantly waved a hand in the air. "It is very well known that a Kumbaya can solve any disagreement." He slid a Twix bar from his pocket, handed it over to me and dropped a slice of jerky on the floor of the porch for Hank, before settling down on the couch. "Where's Tessy?"

"Taking a cat nap."

"Don't let me forget to give her a treat before I leave." He balanced his walking stick against the wall.

"Okay." I ripped the edge of the candy wrapper.

"Let me tell ya a story, Annie."

"Oh, no!"

Huntington, West Virginia
November 12, 1970
Mourning the Herd
{{10}}

The hotdogs were rolled up in a napkin that kept the bun soft and the sauce warm, which is why everyone who lived in Huntington always stopped in to eat at Stewart's Original Hotdogs when they had the chance. Stewart's served up the juiciest hotdogs in all of Huntington and their root beer was as cold and as deliciously frosty as they come. Will pulled into the parking lot and rolled down the driver's side window. His mouth was watering in anticipation of gobbling up the hotdogs smothered with homemade sauce.

A young girl, wearing an orange shirt and bell-bottom jeans, came out to put a ticket number on the windshield. "Welcome to Stewart's. What can I get for ya?"

"Four hotdogs and a root beer, please."

"Onions?" she inquired.

"Absolutely."

"Will that be all?"

"That's all for now," Will chuckled.

The girl wrote the order on a green pad and walked off to stick it on the metal wheel inside.

Will was drumming his fingers on the steering wheel, keeping tune with B.J. Thomas singing "Raindrops Keep Fallin' On My Head" when he heard someone call out his name.

"Hey Will!"

He turned the volume down on the radio and skimmed the lot, where he saw John, the Marshall University football manager, walking towards him.

"Howdy John. How's everything?"

John rested his hand against the hood of the pickup truck. "Everything is going just fine. The Thundering Herd is flying out tomorrow to play a game against the East Carolina Pirates. Everyone is very excited."

"I would say so." Will agreed. "The team doesn't get the opportunity to travel by plane very often. How do ya think they'll do?"

"I think they'll make us proud," John replied.

"Are you lookin' forward to flying down to North Carolina?" Will asked.

"No," John admitted, "I'm not flying down. I'm uncomfortable about flying, so I'm going to transport the Herds football equipment in the back of my truck. However, there are a few extra seats available on the plane, and I can get you a free ticket if you'd like to go to the game."

"Wow," Will scratched his jaw, "that'd be a fun trip." He started thinking about what he had planned for the next few days. "It's short notice though."

"They're leaving tomorrow and flying back on Saturday." John clarified the arrangements. "They were going to cancel the flight, but changed plans and they've chartered a plane with Southern Airways."

"Hmmm..." Will half grunted.

"It would be an opportunity of a lifetime," John added.

"When would I need to let ya know?" Will asked.

"Before the end of the day."

"I might go," Will told him, "let me think on it for a little bit." Suddenly Will recalled a joke he had heard some years back. "John, let me tell ya joke I heard a while ago."

"All right." The man leaned in closer.

"There was an elderly fella who went to the doctor for an

examination. The doctor said, 'You're going to have to give up 'bout half of your love life.' The man asked, 'Which half? Thinking 'bout it? Or talking 'bout it?' " Will started laughing so hard he could hardly catch his breath and John joined along in the merriment.

Finally Will spat out, "Then I started cyphering and started wonderin' why my doctor was telling everyone in town 'bout my love life. That's confidential information."

This comment made them both laugh even harder and they were still chortling out loud when the young girl approached Will's truck carrying a tray full of hotdogs and two frosty mugs of root beer. "Are you fellas eating lunch together?" she asked.

"Sure," John replied.

"Should we take 'em to the dining room?" Will gestured toward the back of the pickup.

"That'd be fine."

Will opened the door, moved around to the rear of his truck, and lowered the tailgate. The waitress sat the tray in the bed of the truck. Will slid her a ten-dollar bill and told her to keep the change. John did the same.

"Thank ya'll," she nodded politely, "just give me a holler if you need anything else."

The two friends lowered down into the back of the truck and looked out over the bare trees. The orange and gold leaves that peek out every autumn had vanished and all that remained was the gloomy stark branches of oak and maple trees.

"Do you like this time of year, Will?" John asked, unwrapping a warm hot dog from its protective napkin.

"Not really," Will told him, "I find it a little depressing. Especially since Lillian passed away around this time last year."

John dipped his chin slightly. "Yeah, I'm sure it's difficult to lose your wife."

They sat in contented silence and washed down their hotdogs with the frothy root beer.

John rested his empty glass down on the tray. "I should get back to work, Will. What about the game? Do you want to go?"

Will swiped a paper napkin across his chili-stained chin. "I'm much obliged. I think I'll take ya up on it. It's a mighty fine offer."

"Great," John reached into his trouser pocket, removed his wallet, and handed Will a ticket. "Maybe I'll see you at the football game."

"Thanks, John."

"No problem," Will could hear John say as he walked away, offering a quick wave over the back of his shoulder.

On the following morning, Will buttoned up his best brown, polyester leisure suit, dabbed a spot of Brylcreem on his hair and slicked it back. He studied his care worn face in the mirror and wondered where the last seventy years had gone. His seventy-eighth birthday had passed a month earlier without fanfare or celebration. He leaned in closer, *"Are those smile lines or wrinkles?"*

He tried to recall the last time he had actually gone anywhere to have fun. He couldn't remember. Since his wife, Lillian, had passed away, his best friend had been Jack Daniels. He momentarily wondered if he should stash a bottle in his pocket and quickly decided he would go on this trip without his constant companion.

He checked his watch, double-checked to make sure he still had his ticket in his billfold, dawdled out to the garage and fired up his truck.

Will had driven a little over three miles, in the drizzling rain, when the engine started making loud thumping noises. *"What in the tarnation?"* He pulled off the road and guided his truck in alongside a muddy stream. He smacked the steering wheel with his fist, wondering why these things always happened to him. *"Great, now I'm going to get soaked in the rain while I fix this cantankerous old jalopy."*

He lifted up the hood and steam poured out from underneath it causing his glasses to fog up. He slammed it down in frustration and decided he would stick out his thumb and try to hitch a ride—if a vehicle passed this way any time soon. He inspected his watch again. "Dag-gone-it! I'm gonna miss the flight."

Will threw open the door and started collecting everything he would need to take with him. He figured if he started walking in the direction he was heading he'd eventually catch a ride. He locked the door and set out on foot.

Will had only walked about ten yards when he heard a booming voice address him. "Don't be afraid!"

He startled and looked to the sky. "Why are ya always sneaking up on me?" He shouted, "You scare the heebie-jeebies out of me every time you suddenly appear like that!"

"Be still."

Will regarded the majestic form for a long moment. "Do ya mean to stay put?"

"Be still," the angel repeated.

Will turned and saw a tractor-trailer approaching him. The driver slowed and hollered out his window, "Hey fellow, do ya need a ride?"

Will once again looked heavenward then directed his attention toward the driver. "No. Thank ya, though."

Will stood, silently bewildered. He watched as the tractor-trailer zoomed down the highway and the clouds parted above him. Then a protective light shone down on him, and across the whole wide deserted highway.

A white feather slowly coasted down from the sky, so he extended his hand and snatched it in midair. "Alrighty then, thank ya," he mumbled before he unlocked the door to his pickup truck, scuttled inside and reluctantly accepted his fate.

Saturday evening, Will tuned in the radio, snuggled up on the sofa and scrutinized the cover of *Love Story* by Erich Segal. The librarian had highly recommended it and assured Will that although it was a bit sad, he would enjoy it. He tentatively opened the book to chapter one. "What can you say about a twenty-five-year-old girl who died? That she was beautiful. And brilliant. That she loved Mozart and Bach." He closed the book impulsively. "I don't think *Love Story* is going to lift my spirits," he said to the bottle of Jack Daniels out of the corner of his watering eye. *"What is wrong with me? I feel like a sappy old man tonight."* He walked to the refrigerator, removed a tray of ice, twisted it firmly to loosen the cubes, and filled a glass with whiskey.

"I'm not going to think 'bout Lillian tonight," he said out loud, although there was no one there to hear him. He turned the knob on the radio to increase the volume.

"Bridge Over Troubled Water" by Simon and Garfunkel started blaring from the side speakers. He exhaled noisily. He took a long, satisfying drink and leaned over to switch stations when he heard the announcement:

"We interrupt this program to bring you breaking news. We have just learned that the plane that was carrying seventy-five members, coaching staff, and boosters of the Marshall University Thundering Herd football team crashed into a hill just short of the Tri-State Airport at approximately 7:30 p.m. this evening. The team was returning home after a 17-14 loss to the East Carolina Pirates at Ficklen Stadium in Greenville, North Carolina and it is believed that all those aboard Southern Airways Flight 932 may have perished when the plane collided with the tops of trees on a hillside and burst into flames. Emergency crews are on the scene. Stay tuned as we keep you updated on this tragic story."

The glass Will was holding slipped from his hand and shattered against the ceramic tile sending hundreds of tiny shards all over the kitchen floor. He gawked, in shock, at the radio. He wondered if he had heard correctly.

"No!" A scream tore from his throat.

He pulled out a chair and rested his head on top of the kitchen table. The agony leapt from his heart, causing his body to convulse. His cries, although muted, were deep and mournful whilst the radio boomed in the background. He mourned for Lillian, he mourned for himself, and most of all he mourned for the families of the seventy-five people on board Southern Airways flight 932. The flight he would have been on had his angel not interceded.

"Why did you spare my life?" he fervently asked God.

There was no response.

Sissonville, West Virginia
September 18, 1981
Kumbaya
{{11}}

At the crack of dawn, way before anyone in their right mind should be out of bed, I awoke only to discover Hank was tugging my quilt off the bed with his teeth.

"Quit it Hank!" I jerked my warm blanket from his clenched teeth.

"Nooo." His head began shaking.

"What is it now?" I peeped at him with one eye open.

His head motioned toward the front of the house.

"Geeze." I slid out of the warm feather bed, wrapped myself in a robe, and followed him to the living room. When I peered through the rectangular glass blocks of the front door, I gasped. "Oh no!"

There I could see, were six women, dressed to impress, piling out of a van. The side of the vehicle clearly identified them as members of The United Methodist Church. I examined my wrinkled pajama pants, worn robe and didn't even need to look in a mirror to realize my hair was a tousled, chaotic mess. "I haven't even brushed my teeth yet, Hank."

"Truue." He shot me a judgmental glance.

I sprinted to the bedroom and ran a quick brush through my hair, dabbed a blob of toothpaste in my mouth, and threw on an old, wrinkled sweatshirt before the knock echoed at the door.

"Good morning," I slung the door open as if I was more than ready to host a formal tea party.

"Good morning." One of the ladies smiled brightly as she

pulled, what remained of, the tattered screen door open. "We are from The United Methodist Church."

My weight shifted uncomfortably and I silently prayed, *"Please don't ask why I haven't been attending church."*

"We've just stopped by to say hello and to see if we could arrange a sort of housewarming party for you. We realize you've just moved in and we would love to help you get organized, and of course we'll be helping Pearl and Will with their wedding plans."

"Please come in." I motioned with my left hand. "Can I fix you ladies a cup of coffee?"

"No." They seemed to share a knowing look.

I briefly wondered if Will or Pearl had relayed my lack of culinary skills to everyone at church, then realized I'd be better off not knowing.

"We've brought up some coffee and muffins."

"We won't be staying long."

The ladies followed me into the living room, settled around on the velvet sofa and miscellaneous chairs before opening thermoses filled with steaming coffee. Paper plates were passed around and a basket of muffins were staunchly placed on the coffee table.

"My name is Betty," the beautiful woman in a red dress introduced herself before continuing, "and this is Cathleen, Joyce, Janet, JoAnn, and Chloe."

"It's very nice to meet you." I forced a smile.

"Erma was a meticulous housekeeper," Betty said.

"Yes, indeed," Joyce agreed.

Janet added, "A very talented decorator too."

"Amen," Chloe confirmed.

My face suffused with color as I reflected on my not-so-lofty housekeeping standards. I wondered if they had noticed the rather large, grotesque hairball Tessy had coughed up in the middle of the floor. *"Do they see that? How could they not?"*

"So," Betty delicately broached, "how was it you ended up buying this farm from Erma?"

"Well, Erma and I were friends and after she passed on over to the sweet by and by I decided to purchase this old place."

"Oh," Joyce cleared her throat, "how did you meet Erma?"

"I was a friend of Ida's and she, sort of, introduced us. Actually, Ida was watching Hank while Erma was at the Cleveland Clinic and asked me to drive him home once Erma returned. I ended up stopping at Will's grocery store at the mouth of Cicerone Route and met him before I met Erma. It was a twist of fate one could say." I skimmed from one interested face to another. "It was a blessing to have made friends with Ida, Erma and Will."

"I see."

"Ida was a sweetheart," Janet remarked.

"Amen," Chloe agreed.

"Are they here to check me out? Are they concerned that the house is falling down due to the lack of daily maintenance?" I impatiently waited for the situation to become transparent as my eyes darted around the room.

Finally Joann explained, "We don't have time to hold a proper housewarming party before the wedding so we decided to spruce up the place for your housewarming and get things ready for Pearl and Will's wedding at the same time. It will take care of two things in one quick sweep."

The bamboozled expression on my face did not go unnoticed. It was pretty obvious that my idea of housework was to sweep the room with a glance.

"Annie," Cathleen assured, "there is no need to be

78

embarrassed about this old farmhouse. We've all been in the same situation at one time or another. Lord have mercy, if you could see the shape of my toilets at home you would cringe."

Joyce nodded in agreement. "If you stopped by my house all you would see is a decade of rescued books piled up to the ceiling. I'm half tempted to sort through them but can never find the time."

"We just felt it would help you out if we took a look around, notated what might be done to help get ready for the big day, and bring the supplies over and simply spruce everything up." Her eyes opened wide in anticipation. "Do you mind if we take a look around to see what might need done?"

My lips formed a flat straight line as I carefully deliberated upon their proposal. "That would be fine," I finally sputtered out, "as long as you don't touch Erma's clinic."

"No, we'll just close the door leading to her clinic."

I added as an afterthought, "Or the attic."

"No problem," Betty promised.

I reluctantly consented, "Okay."

"Is there anything particular that you would like us to take care of?"

My eyes immediately dropped to the velvet couch where I noticed poor Joyce now had Hank's hair covering the seat of her perfectly creased black dress slacks. "I've been meaning to buy a cover for this sofa."

"Of course."

"I've also pondered on whether I should take the couch on the front porch to the dump."

Chloe eyed me suspiciously. "No. It looks comfy. It must be a great place to relax and watch the sun go down."

"Yeah, that's what Will said too…" I paused transitorily, "there was recently an accident, or incident may be a better word, and the screen door was shattered." My mouth twitched. "It's going to need replaced."

"These are all wonderful ideas, Annie. Perfect!" Janet enthusiastically interjected.

"Our plan is to just put a little lipstick on the pig," Joann chimed in.

"Spruce up the place a little," Joyce added.

"Renew your look," Cathleen inserted.

"One call cleans it all," Betty giggled at her own clever addition.

"We won't feed the dust bunnies," Chloe teased as she patted my knee.

"Sure…" I embarrassedly agreed.

"Great. We'll be up here on Monday morning."

"I start to work on Monday." I faked regret.

"Not a problem. Do you care to leave the door unlocked?"

I was speechless.

Janet, seemingly understanding my reluctance interjected, "We are members of The United Methodist Church so all of your belongings will be intact when you come home."

"Oh," now I was mortified, "that is not what I meant. My only concern is that Hank and my cat, Tessy, will be up here and may get in your way." I spoke casually but inside I was shaking with a mixture of embarrassment, and sheer astonishment at my loudmouthed stupidity.

Hank, as if on cue, sauntered over, dropped down in the middle of the floor, and shamelessly exposed his belly to the room full of visitors.

The women tittered and chuckled out loud.

"Isn't he adorable?" Janet chortled.

"A real gem," I murmured underneath my breath.

"Great, we'll be up here Monday morning to take care of everything."

Then just as suddenly as they had appeared they disappeared, leaving me wondering, *"What exactly did I just agree to?"*

On Monday, at the end of my first day of working as a psychologist, I parked my Volkswagen at the end of the gravel driveway in front of the old farmhouse. I gawked at it for a long spell, wondering if I might be at the wrong house.

A new, brown, weatherproof covering was draped over top of the decaying plaid couch. I could see from the vantage point where I was parked, that the splintered screen door, which Hank had lugged me through, had been replaced.

The large front lawn had been mowed and it appeared the sticks, dried-up walnut shell, and broken limbs in the yard, had been removed and disposed of. Even the stray whirlybirds had been removed from the gutters.

I plucked the keys from the ignition, strolled to the front porch and noticed a few dozen pots filled with pungent, auburn geraniums crammed safely in the corner.

When I pushed open the front door, Hank and Tessy came running toward me with eager expressions daubing their endearing faces. Tessy started jabbering something I did not understand then Hank butted in with his incomprehensible version of what exactly had taken place while I was gone.

The blue velvet sofa had been vacuumed and a floral runner had been swathed over the seat cushions. I poked around—curiously wondering exactly which of the undesirable tasks the ladies from The United Methodist Church had chosen to tackle. *"No hairballs. No dust bunnies. No brown water spots clinging to the window. Wow! This place looks great."* I scanned the clinic area that Erma had used when she was a veterinarian and it hadn't been touched. *"Just as they promised."*

Hank released a barely audible sound, reminiscent of a bark, and I froze to listen. I could hear Will's pickup truck dodging the ruts of the willowy dirt path leading up the mountaintop.

"Will's coming," I told Hank and Tessy.

Hank jiggled enthusiastically.

"He probably has Pearl and Buster with him," I reminded Hank.

"Humph!" he snorted before sauntering into the kitchen.

"Come on, Hank. You know that we have discussed this issue. We are going to go greet our company and you better behave." I glared at him through narrowed eyes. "I mean it."

He ignored me, dropped down in the corner of kitchen floor, and curled up into a tight ball.

When Will's battered truck peeked through the thick forest at the top of the mountain, Tessy and I were out there to greet them.

"Where's Hank?" Will asked as he walked to the passenger side door and opened it allowing Buster and Pearl to pile out.

"Hiding in the kitchen."

Will's mouth turned up in a half smile. "He probably doesn't realize that I brought him some JERKY!" he shouted out the last word.

The word jerky was indeed enough to coax the ole dog to the front porch. His sad, accusing eyes drooped as he pushed open the front door.

I noticed Buster freeze. He started shaking.

"It's alright, Buster," Pearl said. Her voice was gentle, like a doctor giving bad news. She grasped both of his hands. "We talked about meeting Hank again. Do you remember? Hank is my very dear friend."

Buster's face flushed choleric and his shoulders slumped.

"I brought everyone their favorite treat. I was figurin' we could have a little picnic snack out here on the lawn," Will announced.

"I could cook us something quick if anyone wants dinner," I volunteered.

"Nooo." Hank shook his head firmly.

Pearl provided a petite shake of her head indicating that she wasn't interested in having me cook dinner.

"Absolutely not!" Will shot Pearl a knowing look before clarifying, "I went to a great deal of trouble packing everyone's favorite treats."

"Whatever," I mumbled.

"Yep. I have beef jerky for Hank, a Granny Smith apple for Buster, an entire pouch of tuna flavored tidbits for Tessy, Little Debbie cakes for Pearl and I, and of course, a Twix bar for you."

Pearl interjected, "And I brought us a blanket to sit on."

"A picnic it is." I drew her attention toward the large walnut tree. "Would you like to lounge in the shade?"

"That would be perfect."

Will, Pearl, and Buster slowly ambled toward the tree, while Hank, Tessy, and I followed behind at a safe distance. Hank's face was stubbornly fixed in a comical sort of shape that put me in mind of an infant refusing to taste liquefied peas.

After Pearl spread out the colorful patchwork blanket, we settled down and Pearl afforded introductions. "Buster, this is my best canine friend in the whole world." Her hand rose to cover her heart. "Could you say hello to Hank, please?"

"Howdy, Hank."

Hank ignored him.

"Hank," Pearl cooed, "this is my new friend Buster."

"Humph!"

I rubbed Hank's head and whispered in his big, floppy ear, "Be nice."

Will handed everyone their designated treats and when Buster held his Granny Smith apple out and asked, "Hank, would ya like a bite of my apple?" the hound dog stared at him in astonishment. He appeared to process this gesture carefully, because he crooked his head sideways for a minute, snagged a beef jerky between his teeth, took three steps forward and dropped the dehydrated slice of meat into Buster's lap.

"Awe, isn't he sweet." Pearl smiled from ear to ear.

Buster picked up the slobber-covered hunk of dried beef and took a big bite.

I winced and my nose involuntarily scrunched up in disgust. *"Geeze."*

Pearl cringed.

"See," Will pointed at me, "what did I tell ya? Ya don't need a leash. A good ole fashioned Kumbaya will take care of any ill-feelings."

I calculatedly rolled my eyes at him.

He let out a big belly laugh. "Let me tell ya'll a joke." He glanced around to make sure everyone was listening. "A fella took a dog into a bar and announced that it could talk. The bartender asked what he could say. The man said, 'What's your name?' and the dog said, 'Ruff, ruff.' The man replied, 'That's right Ruff. How are things?' The dog said, 'Ruff, ruff.' The man said, 'You're right. Now, who is the greatest baseball player of all time?' 'Ruff, ruff,' the dog said. The man said, 'That's right, Babe Ruth,' whereupon the bartender threw them out. When they got outside, the dog turned to the man and said, 'I knew I should have said Mickey Mantle.' "

Will started chortling and smacking his leg joyfully. Pearl joined in giggling, Hank rolled around on the ground snickering jubilantly, and even little Tessy appeared to be tittering blissfully. Buster didn't make any sounds but his wide smile told me all I needed to know.

"You are a hoot, Will." I nudged him. "Where do you come up with all of these jokes?"

"Oh, here and there." He snorted under his breath before popping a wad of Mail Pouch in his jaw.

I suddenly recalled that I hadn't told Pearl about the housewarming cleaning that the ladies from The United Methodist Church had so kindly bestowed upon me. "Pearl, the ladies from the church were up here today and they cleaned all kinds of things up, both inside and outside. They are miracle workers."

She smiled brightly. "They came up here today? That is wonderful. Let me take a look around." Her attention turned to Buster, "Would you like to take a walk with me?"

He consented with a slight nod, indicating he would accompany her.

"Hank," Pearl patted his head, "would you like to join us?"

"Yeahh." He stood on all fours and sprayed the blanket

with slobbering dribbles as his body shook all over like a runner preparing for a marathon.

The three of them took off in the direction of the barn, slowly meandering amongst the radiant autumn foliage on the mountaintop.

"Let me ask you something, Will," I said when they were out of earshot, "how was it you ended up buying the grocery store at the end of the road?" My eyes opened wide in anticipation. "Did it have anything to do with Erma living here?"

He gazed at me hesitantly then spat a mouth full of thick, dark liquid into a plastic cup, the spittle dribbling down his chin as he swiped it up using the cup's edge as a catchall. He winked at me. "Well, it's a heartwarming story."

"Heartwarming?" I ran my hand through my hair. *"Geeze."*

Sissonville, West Virginia
March 8, 1975
Hot Toddies with Erma
{{12}}

Will sat, for a long spell, at the mouth of a muddy trail named Black Hollow Road trying to decide, *"Should I surprise Erma with an impromptu visit?"*

He recalled the day when he had met Erma for the first time. It was July 4th at Luna Park. He was working in the booth selling *Tickets for Special Entertainment* and she was visiting Luna Park for the very first time with her friend Ida. The moment he saw her he was awestruck. She was the prettiest girl he had ever seen and when she smiled at him it made his heart sing. Erma told him that she and Ida would be back later for the fireworks and he had all intentions of finding her that night.

"Oh, how I wanted to impress her," he recalled vividly. His thoughts drifted back in time to the specific evening. In a three-story, brick boarding house on the East Side of Charleston, he had ironed his shirt just like his mama had taught him, slid on his best trousers, and splashed a liberal amount of Clubman aftershave on his face and neck. He wrapped up a slab of bologna, hoping they might have a picnic, and gulped down a pint full of moonshine before filling up his flask. *"That was way back in 1915 but it only seems like yesterday."*

Fully realizing that their first meeting had taken place sixty years earlier, and that Erma may not even remember it, he turned the ignition on.

Then he clicked it off again.

He thought about all the letters he had written to Erma

while he was serving in the war and about the kind correspondences she had sent back to him. He wondered if he should tell her that he had kept every single letter she had ever written to him, and that they were still safely tucked away in an old cigar box at home. *"Nah, I won't tell her. She'll think I'm crazy for keepin' all them letters all these years."*

Will saw a single white feather drifting down from the sky.

It glided for a long spell, almost as if it was dancing, turning, pirouetting in the wind, until it came to an abrupt stop—right smack dab on the windshield of his pickup.

"It's a sign," he presumed, so he fired his old truck up and inched forward, dodging the ruts and potholes heading up a mountain that shadowed a willowy dirt path—the very trail that led straight to his beloved Erma.

When he reached the top of the mountain he saw Erma seated on the front porch. She was waving at him enthusiastically. Will was as pleased as punch when he saw her welcoming face.

"Will, how are you?" Erma stretched out her arms and gave him a heartfelt, welcoming hug.

"Just checkin' on you. How are ya doing?"

"I'm fine," she motioned for him to come on in. "Let's catch up, my dear friend."

Will stepped into a cozy living room with large windows overlooking the mountains. He followed her through a wide hallway and into the kitchen where Erma gestured in the direction of the chair.

"Please have a seat, Will. Can I fix you something to drink?" She picked up a teapot, placed it on the stove and twisted the knob to ignite the gas burner. "Would you like a Hot Toddy?"

"I don't drink anymore," Will replied.

"Really?" She turned to face him before asking, "Not at all?"

His response came in the form of a lopsided grin.

Erma bent to look underneath the sink and produced a bottle of brandy. "Hot Toddies are my specialty," she explained. She placed the lemon juice and honey on the countertop.

"Well Erma, if they're your specialty then how can I say no?"

"Exactly." She proceeded to find two large coffee mugs and leaned against the countertop. "So, what brings you all the way out to Sissonville?"

"I was out this way takin' care of some business," he fibbed.

"Oh." She splashed a shot of brandy in a mug. "Single shot or double?"

"Double, please."

Erma giggled appreciatively before filling the mugs with hot water and tendering one to him. She plopped down on a kitchen chair, cupped her warm mug in both hands and took a sip. "What kind of business do you have out here? You're not thinking about buying the grocery store at the end of the road are you?"

Even though he wasn't aware the store was for sale, he was glad she brought the subject up. It gave him a solid alibi—an excellent excuse for his spur-of-the-moment visit. "I'm not sure. What do ya know 'bout it?"

"All I know is that Mr. Dixon passed away and his wife is too ill to take care of it. All of their children have moved out of state so there's no one to tend to it anymore. It's a shame really. It must do good business since it's the only store within a ten mile radius." Erma's eyes widened as though something just occurred to her. "Mr. Dixon used to work on automobiles in the back room too. Do you still tinker around with cars?"

He eyed her ruminatively for a second. "Sometimes."

"Well, it might be a good investment for you to consider." Erma ran her fingertip around the edge of her cup.

Will scrunched his lip in deliberation.

"They have a wonderful produce section. The Dixons bought all of their fruit and vegetables from Dawson's farm and they are always fresh. I wouldn't buy my produce from anyone other than the Dixons. I do hope the new owner doesn't change anything." She peeked over the rim of her mug. "Did you see the produce section when you stopped in the store?"

"No. I haven't stopped in yet. I decided to come up and visit with you first."

"I am so glad you did." Erma reached over and gave him a spry pat on his hand. "Tell me, what have you been up to?"

"I've been retired for a few years and it's starting to get on my nerves a little. I need to do something." He expounded, "It's funny, Erma, but it's like I've always dreamed of retirement and now that I'm retired I don't know how to spend my time."

Erma enthusiastically agreed. "I know what you mean, Will. I'm still doctorin' animals," she leaned in close and confided, "and occasionally people, but don't mention that to anyone—if ya know what I mean. I figure I'll still be working until I'm pushing up daisies."

Will laughed out loud. "Let me tell ya a joke."

"Let me fix *you* another toddy."

Erma stood and Will commenced with his storytelling. "A woman went into a pet shop looking for a pet. She saw this frog that winked at her and made a kissing sound. She went on and looked at the kittens, puppies, and birds, and then she went back to the frog. It winked at her and made a kissing sound again. She thought that was cute, and so she bought it. Driving home, she took him out of his box and set him on the seat beside her. When she peeped down, it again winked at her and made the kissing sound. She leaned over and kissed it, and lo, it turned into a handsome prince!" Will started chuckling before he could spit out the punch line. "And the woman turned into a motel!"

Erma cackled out loud and finally sputtered, "You are ornery, Will!"

After Will settled down from his self-imposed fit of hilarity, he replied, "Yep, I still am." He transferred his weight in the seat causing the chair to moan in response. "Hey Erma, do you remember the first day we met?"

"Of course."

"It was a long time ago, wasn't it?"

"Way back in 1915." Erma contemplated the timeline for a second, "It was sixty years ago."

Will gazed longingly into her eyes. "I fell in love with ya the moment I first laid eyes on ya," he confessed.

"Oh, Will," Erma's face permeated with color and she waved her hand dismissively, "we were just kids."

"Kids or not, you were my first love." His eyes lowered and he stared into the coffee mug for a long drawn out moment, a hint of sadness stealing across his face. "I guess I'll always love ya, Erma. I've cherished ya all my life..."

His confession was abruptly interrupted when the hound dogs started barking out a high-pitched alert. Erma rushed to the front door to see what all the commotion was about and saw Old Man Minor stumbling out of his truck. He ran to the passenger's side of his red Ford and lifted a German shepherd into his arms. "King's been hit by a car," the man shouted out as he plodded to the porch.

"Bring him on in," Erma held the door open wide, "tell me what happened."

Will could overhear the intruder telling Erma his story as she shuffled them into the makeshift veterinarian clinic.

"I'll see myself out, Erma," Will yelled, snatching up his cane.

"I'm sorry, Will. Please come again to visit."

"I'll be back," he promised.

Will pushed the gearshift into "Reverse," turned his truck around at the bend, and bumped down the rutted road.

"I reckon I'm gonna buy me a grocery store," he said to himself—a cunning grin slowly formed when he considered the possibilities.

Sissonville, West Virginia
October 2, 1981
Coons in the Kitchen
{{13}}

I awoke from a romantic dream in which Bob was adoringly kissing me only to discover Hank was licking my face with his slippery, oversized, rough, slimy tongue. "Seriously, Hank! What do you want?"

I could hear Will's truck bouncing up the furrowed road leading up to the farm. I rolled over, allowed my eyes to focus and saw it was five-thirty in the morning. "Geeze, what does he want at this time in morning?"

I sat up and was acutely, painfully aware that my starry-eyed encounter with Bob was a dream, and my reality was right here, snuggled in beside a slobbering, stinking hound dog. I got up, threw on my robe, and hobbled, barefoot to the front door. I snapped the lock and flung the door open wide.

Within a couple of minutes Will was traipsing through the door. The lumbering man was balancing a large cake in his arms.

"I figured I'd bring the wedding cake up this morning."

"At five-thirty? Couldn't it wait until... I don't know, maybe nine o'clock?"

"Nah," he tilted his head toward the cake, "where do ya want me to put it?"

I clamped my lips together to keep from screaming. "In the kitchen, I guess."

"I'll brew us some coffee while you get dressed."

"Dressed for what?"

"I wanna run up to Beane Cemetery this morning and

visit Erma."

"Will, please explain why I need to get dressed in order for you to run up to the cemetery." My head tilted in anticipation of his response.

"Ya do wanna go with me, don't ya?"

"Will you sing the song 'In the Sweet By and By'?"

"Will you accompany me?"

I wasn't sure if he meant accompany him in song or physically driving up to the cemetery, but since it didn't matter one way or the other, I agreed. "Sure."

Will moseyed into the kitchen with Hank and Tessy following at his heels. I heard the thunk of pipes and gush of water as he rinsed the filter basket, spooned in enough grounds for a pot, and filled the carafe.

"Do ya want any breakfast?" I heard him call out.

"Nope." I slid on my jeans and rummaged around for a clean T-shirt. "Could you feed Hank and Tessy for me?"

"Got it!"

By the time I had dressed, brushed my teeth, washed my face, twisted my hair into a ponytail and poked it under a ball cap, the coffee was ready.

"Will," I looked him over, "why are you wearing your best suit to visit the cemetery? It can be muddy walking up the hill."

"I want to look my best when I visit Erma's grave."

"You do realize that Erma won't be able to see you, right?"

"How do ya know?" he shot a pointed glance in my direction.

I accepted defeat. "You're right. I don't know."

I glimpsed longingly in the direction of the sofa where Tessy snored in happy oblivion, and snapped my fingers in the direction of the ole hound dog. "Let's go, Hank, you're going with us."

Hank and I followed Will out to his pickup. Hank leapt in the bed and I slid in the passenger's seat for the short drive up to Beane Cemetery. Will stopped at the mouth of the road leading up the winding hill, slid the gearshift into "Park," and turned to face me.

"If it's alright with you, I rather spend a little time with Erma alone. I wanna have a private talk with her."

"Okay. Do you want me to wait here with Hank?"

"Yep, that'd be great. Maybe ya can join us in 'bout twenty minutes." He slid out of the truck, grabbed his cane and a bouquet of wildflowers before directing Hank to stay put.

As I watched him dawdle up the path, my mouth turned up in a half smile when I noticed him pluck a stray feather from midair. It appeared, from my vantage point, that an angel's protective light was shining down directly on him as he disappeared around the bend in the road. Hank and I settled in on the tailgate and it wasn't long until we could hear Will singing "In the Sweet By and By." He crooned like the birds sing, not worrying about who hears or what they think. His rich, deep baritone voice echoed, resonating beautifully throughout the whole immense valley.

Shortly thereafter, Hank and I joined Will. I helped hoist him from the ground, ignored the tears that were streaming down his cheeks, and gave him a gentle rub on the arm. "Are you ready to go?"

"I reckon."

I said hello to Erma and to her best friend Ida, noticing that Will had placed flowers on each of their graves, and we took our good ole sweet time walking off the mountain, down the winding path, and to the truck.

"Would you like me to drive us home?" I offered,

assuming he may not feel like driving right at the moment.

Will glared at me, scrunched his nose up, and deliberately informed me, "That makes as much sense as a trapdoor in a canoe."

"Fine." I threw my hands up in the air.

"Ain't nobody drivin' my pickup truck except me," I heard him mumble to Hank as I climbed in the cab.

I could see, through the rearview mirror, when Hank's eyes shot to the heavens indicating that my suggestion to drive us home was, indeed, the silliest thing he had ever heard.

We were on the road for several minutes before I blurted out, "Why did you tell me your stories, Will?"

"What stories?" he questioned.

"The stories about your angel."

"I want to make your passage through life easier than mine."

"So, the stories concerning the fawn, the war, the bridge collapsing, the plane crash, feathers and dreams were meant to make my passage through life easier."

"Yep." My friend shot me a sideways glance. "You're not always the brightest bulb on the tree so I figured I'd give ya some help. Some things ya need to remember are," he shot up his pointer finger, "one, when angels are near feathers appear."

"Got it," I said.

Finger number two whipped up dramatically. "When an angel tells ya to be still, then ya best be still."

"Be still," I repeated.

He continued, "Never hurt anything without a purpose. Help others when ya can and always, I mean always, listen when angels talk to ya, because 'we cannot pass our guardian angel's bounds, resigned or sullen, he will hear our sighs.' Do you know who said that quote?"

"Age had not addled his brain," I silently gauged. "No." I stared at him incredulously, "I don't even know what that means, Will."

"That Ph.D. helped ya out a lot, didn't it Annie?"

My lower lip shot out in a pout. "I am a psychologist, and I think you are disturbed."

"I'll tell ya who said that," he intentionally ignored me, "Saint Augustine was the bearer of those wise words," Will added confidently, "and Saint Augustine was a smart man."

He confessed this with such authority that I had to jab, "Did you know him personally?"

Will grunted grumpily.

"Okay," I mused. "What does 'we cannot pass our guardian angel's bounds, resigned or sullen, he will hear our sighs' actually mean?"

"Lord have mercy, Annie! It simply *means* that our angels are *always* with us, whether we are submissive and accepting or bad-tempered and surly, they still are watching over us and protecting us." I heard him murmur under his breath, "Goodness gracious."

It was an interesting notion, and the more that I thought about it the more intriguing it became. "Alright then, angel expert, tell me this—are angels gender specific?"

"Gender specific? What in the tarnation are ya talkin' 'bout?"

"Do boys have male angels and girls have female angels?"

"I have no idea." He seemed to ponder this judiciously. "Why do you ask?"

I recalled a passage I had read in Erma's journal.

Erma felt a tug at her sleeve and glimpsed down to

see a small girl, her long brown braid flowing down her back. The dark circles under her eyes caused a twinge of sympathy to stir deep within Erma's heart.

"Can I have one of those?" the child asked as she pointed toward the oranges.

"An orange? Sure," Erma stretched down and handed one to the child, "would ya like a sandwich?"

"No," the little girl answered, "I've never had an orange before and I was just wonderin' what they tasted like."

Erma recalled the fate of those living in a mining town, and from her own life experiences knew perfectly well there was always a lack of fresh fruit available in company-owned stores. "You're gonna love it." She offered a wink. She demonstrated how to peel the orange and the little girl sat down beside her on the blanket. "Poor child," Erma thought, "is gonna be without a father – just like I was."

"What's your name?" Erma asked.

"Cathy," the little girl responded as she shoved a slice of the citrus treat into her mouth.

"Is your daddy in there?" Erma pointed toward the mine.

"Yep," she grinned, "but he's gonna come out any minute."

Erma gently patted the child's arm. "I do hope so," she said encouragingly, as she smoothed at the wrinkles that were forming on her forehead.

"He will," the child nodded her head confidently, "the angel told me so."

"The angel?" Erma's eyes widened.

"Yep," Cathy pointed toward the top of the mountain. "She said, 'don't be afraid.' "

Erma's gaze followed the direction of the child's pointed finger. She froze and stared. "Sure enough," Erma gulped, "it looks like an angel hovering above the mine over there. Nah, it couldn't be." She squinted her eyes in an effort to get a better look, "Could it be?"

Erma twisted around to face the child, "Did ya talk back to her?"

"Sure," she tilted her head slightly, "I said thank ya."

"Of course," Erma replied as the child suddenly dropped her orange to the ground and took off running toward the mine. A man stumbled out from the bowels of the dark pit, coughing up the black dust that had tainted his lungs, and the little girl threw her arms around his waist.

Erma gazed at the top of the mountain again, only to witness the apparition vanish in front of her eyes. "It must be residue from the coal dust plume that forms after a mine explodes," she reasoned, as she thought it all through. She looked up toward heaven only to spy a tiny glimmer of sunshine peeping through a vertical slit in the clouds. "Or an angel," she reconsidered.

"When I was reading Erma's journal she had written about a little girl who saw an angel outside of a mining accident and the little girl referred to the angel as *she*. So, I just wondered how angels were assigned and whether or not they were appointed to humans according to their gender."

"I don't have a clue," Will earnestly replied. He rubbed his jaw for a second, "I can't quite be one hundred percent sure 'bout that."

"Okay. Why do you think they say, 'Don't be afraid' when addressing humans?"

"Ah," he nodded convincingly, "I do have a theory 'bout that. I don't think they're always saying don't be afraid of the situation. I think sometimes they're sayin' don't be afraid of them, because heavenly angels are so splendid, so enormous, and so brilliant that when ya first see one it's a bit overwhelming. The glow that surrounds them is so bright that ya have to turn away for a second to allow your eyes to refocus. They kinda startle ya, if ya know what I mean." He glanced at me for a second before directing his attention back to the highway. "Now earthly angels are a horse of different color because ya don't know them until they are gone, plus they just walk around looking like the rest of us. However, heavenly angels unquestionably demand your attentiveness and they leave ya in awe. You'll know it when ya see one, for sure."

When we reached the top of Black Hollow Road, Will turned the ignition off and asked, "Do ya understand everything I've told ya 'bout angels?"

"I hope so." I smiled at him convincingly.

"Good." He added a single nod of his head. "Don't forget it."

"Here is another question, Will, do you know your angel's name?"

"No," Will replied evenly, "he didn't take the time to introduce himself."

"I was just wondering."

I noticed the creases in Will's cheeks deepen to slashes when his mouth turned up in a half grin. "You ask the silliest questions sometimes, Annie."

I ignored his comment. "This is the *very* last question, Will. I promise. Do you think your angel has ever asked, 'What in the tarnation has he done now?' "

"No, but I'm sure your angel is constantly asking that

very question."

I responded by slamming the truck door shut with great force.

The three of us walked slowly toward the large wraparound porch and Will and Hank stood patiently waiting for me to find my key and unlock the front door. I threw it open for them to enter. The moment Hank stepped over the threshold he wailed, *"Nooo!"* and scurried toward the kitchen. His nails scrabbled down the hall and slid to a stop outside the kitchen door.

Will and I followed in his wake. My heartbeat quickened and my gut twisted into a tight ball when I heard the clanking and clattering. I shoved the door open and Hank barreled into the kitchen. He started barking out a deafening forewarning.

"What is going on?" I looked at Will sideways.

We peered through the door and spied a plump raccoon perched on the kitchen table; one of her hands was clutching a plastic cake-topper and the other scooping up bits of white icing. She froze when we entered.

My eyes darted around the room and saw three baby raccoons feasting on clumps of cake by the kitchen sink.

"I must have left the window open."

"Yep," Will concurred.

I addressed the hefty raccoon in my most beguiling tone, "Don't be afraid. We won't hurt you."

Hank growled.

Just for a few seconds the large raccoon glared at me, her great brilliant eyes full of hate then she wound tightly into a ball.

"It's okay," I scanned the room again. This time I was searching for Tessy. She was calmly sitting by the back door. Her broad green eyes regarded me innocently.

For something like a third of a second the coiled creature who was eating the wedding cake observed Hank tensely, then a masked black body exploded silently from the table past Hank's left ear on to the top of the refrigerator and in an instant set off on a whirlwind circuit of the room; along the tops of cupboards, across the curtains, careering round and round like Richard Petty at a NASCAR race.

Poor little Tessy startled by the scattering of plates and tins and pans, and by Hank howling at the top of his lungs, began to run around in turn, knocking over the water dish on the floor, and sliding through the trash that had been toppled over earlier, most likely before the clan of raccoons had detected the wedding cake.

The smaller raccoons watched pensively until their mama performed one last breathtaking leap—like a trapeze artist at the circus she sprung from the small corner cupboard, causing it to topple to the floor, and landed gracefully on the narrow windowsill.

The sound of glassware breaking distracted Hank momentarily.

Then, one by one the baby raccoons bounced like uncoiled springs through the partly open window and shot into the back yard. The thick-set mama waited until each of her little ones escaped before she turned to face us, wiped a mass of white icing from her mouth, turned victoriously and bolted through the ajar window.

We watched them, our jaws gaping open, as they scampered out of sight.

Will, Hank, Tessy and I examined one another's eyes for a long moment before our eyes settled on Tessy. She guiltily dropped her gaze to the floor.

Finally, in a moment of great clarity, I offered up, "I'll bake a sheet cake."

"Pearl is gonna kill me, Annie." Will threw his hands up in the air. "The wedding is tomorrow!"

"She won't *kill* you," I consoled him, "you'll just wish she had."

"Can we repair the cake?" Will asked.

We both despondently ogled the remains intently.

"The head of the groom is well... well, it's gone, Will." I poked the edge of the once beautifully decorated piece of art. "They ate at least half of it."

"I can see that, Annie."

"I'll bake a sheet cake," I suggested again, pushing a strand of hair out of my eyes.

"And risk everyone getting the trots?" Will shuddered as he said it.

Being fairly quick-witted, I picked up on his sarcasm. "What *exactly* are you insinuating?"

"I ain't insinuating nothin'. You are a terrible cook."

I suppressed a groan. "It's a sheet cake, Will," I spat through clinched teeth, "it comes in a box. All I have to do is add eggs and pop it into the oven."

"So what, pray tell, are we gonna do 'bout the bride and groom cake-toppers?" Will inquired agitatedly.

I bit my lip as I thought it all through. "We'll put Little Debbie cakes on the top. Do you have any on you?"

"Yep, I have some Swiss Rolls and Banana Twins out in the truck."

"You didn't steal one of Pearl's Swiss Rolls, did you?"

"I did," he confessed.

"Why?"

"I just wanted to irritate her a little bit 'cause that's what married folks do."

"Pretty lame excuse."

A wide smile covered his face. "I'll go fetch 'em."

I pointed my finger at him. "I don't know why she puts up with you."

He turned to leave the kitchen, snickering under his breath.

"Hey Will," I called after him, "where did Pearl hide the Little Debbie Cakes?"

He chuckled, "She stashed 'em in the clothes dryer."

"Geeze."

Sissonville, West Virginia
October 3, 1981
Holy Matrimony
{{14}}

When I heard the first vehicle bouncing up Black Hollow Road, I opened the door onto the bright, innocent yellow and crimson of autumn foliage. Will and I had spent the previous evening cleaning up after the 'coons in the kitchen disaster, and we had even situated each pot of pungent, auburn geraniums strategically around the porch. I glanced around the house and yard and felt proud, and a little surprised, that the old farmhouse cleaned up so nicely. I pressed the imaginary creases out of the skirt on my carroty-colored bridesmaid dress, and straightened up the brown, weatherproof covering that swathed the decomposing plaid couch.

Will started tooting his horn before he reached the top of the mountaintop and by the time he reached the peak I was out there to greet him.

"Are you ready, Will?" I asked, as he slung open the door to his truck.

"I'm as ready as a rooster in a hen house."

"You best get the preacher up here before you start thinking about that," I informed him matter-of-factly.

"Good one, Annie." He pulled his walking stick out and balanced it on the ground. "I came up a little early to help ya get things tidied up."

"Everything is perfect. There's nothing left to do but to say *I do*."

He glared at me over the top of his glasses. "You're full of wisecracks today aren't ya?"

"Yes, I'm very happy for you." I wrapped my arms around him.

"Thank ya," he whispered in my ear.

"My only concern, Will, is whether you will continue to come up and visit me after the wedding."

"Are ya kiddin' me?" He patted me on the back. "You're gonna still need my help around the farm. After all, who else do ya know that can rewire a house with nothing more than a dull butter knife and a roll of duct tape?"

I closed my eyes and tried to think. Finally I confessed, "I don't know anyone else who possesses the multitude of proficiencies that you do."

"You are a good friend."

"You too," I replied.

It wasn't long until folks started arriving for the wedding ceremony, and each came bearing comfort food, as this is a longstanding tradition for mountain folk. (We always rejoice with those who do rejoice and mourn with those who mourn.) There were platters full of country-fried chicken, baked turkey, roasted pork, meatballs, dressing, candied yams, green beans, creamed corn, broccoli casserole, cheesy potatoes, fluffy yeast rolls, corn muffins and pumpkin rolls covering every inch of uninhabited space in the kitchen. Coach Dave even lugged in a cooler he had borrowed from the Sissonville High School football team that filled to the brim with sweet tea.

I quickly discerned that although Pearl had indicated there would be only twenty or so people in attendance, I easily counted sixty-five folks or more—and it didn't matter one iota.

Hank, who was Will's best man, had been bathed (which coincidentally, was the first time I tasted soap) and was stylishly donning a large orange bowtie that was connected by a clip to his collar.

Hank and Will sauntered to the front lawn and positioned themselves underneath the large walnut tree in front of Pastor Goodman, and shortly thereafter the guests started slowly meandering in that direction. Once everyone had found a place to stand, so they could witness the ceremony, I heard Betty, Cathleen, Joyce, Janet, JoAnn, and Chloe, from The United Methodist Church choir, start singing a glorious rendition of "Amazing Grace."

"Are you ready, Pearl?"

She nodded shakily.

"Lets' go," I said with a smile.

She nuzzled her arm through Buster's arm and slowly walked across the rippling meadow and through the crowd of well-wishers. The music continued, and with her head held high and a grin on her face, Pearl promenaded toward her handsome groom. Grace was in her steps, and heaven in her eyes.

Standing around the lawn were our friends, neighbors, and the entire congregation of The United Methodist Church. There were dozens of children and dogs running everywhere—all present to serve as witnesses to the bride and groom's oath of Holy Matrimony.

As Pearl stood beside Will and they exchanged their vows, I saw the love beaming on Pearl's face. Buster had the honor of "giving her away," and I just stood there smiling brightly, sporting my bright orange carroty-colored dress.

When the ceremony was over Will kissed her. Then Pastor Goodman introduced them as husband and wife and what followed was a moment of sustained applause before rowdy remarks rang out from the crowd.

The very moment that the Pastor said, "Bless the bride,

bless the bowl, bless the biscuits, and give 'em soul. There's plenty of food in the farmhouse. Ya'll go help your selves," I heard Bob's Jeep zooming up the hollow. I was smiling from ear to ear when he came to a screeching halt, jumped out of the Jeep and ran toward me.

"Annie, I'm so sorry. I missed the ceremony didn't I?"

"Yes, but it is no problem. I'm just glad you made it. It was a sweet ceremony and we all know that a fine beginning makes a dandy ending." I nudged him. "We're getting ready to have the reception, come on in." I gave him a quick peck on his cheek and Hank barked enthusiastically in an attempt to divert Bob's attention toward him.

"Hey Hank," Bob pulled a butterscotch candy from his pocket and threw it up in the air, "you make a very handsome best man." The ole hound dog leapt up and caught the hard candy like he had been professionally trained to perform for the Ringling Brothers and Barnum & Bailey Circus.

I knitted my arm through Bob's and began introducing him to the fine folks who had come to celebrate this momentous occasion with my friends.

Plates were filled with vegetables, meats, fruits, and casseroles and everyone found a seat wherever they could. After about an hour, Will announced it was time to gather at the punch bowl so everyone snuggled in tight around a table, on the large wraparound porch, and Will removed the plastic Tupperware top that had once displayed an ornate, traditional stack-cake and handed it over to me.

Pearl was mighty surprised when the wedding cake was revealed, I could tell by the fleeting expression of terror that enveloped her face. However, she faltered for only a split second before a wide smile wrapped up around her cheeks. I knew she was anticipating seeing a beautifully crafted, round, three-tier wedding cake with an adoring bride and groom gloriously nestled on the top, but as a replacement sat an oblong sheet cake that was liberally covered with lumpy frosting and two Little Debbie Snack Cakes.

After the bride and groom cut the cake, Will attempted to snatch the Swiss Roll from the top, only to get his hand swatted. He released a good old belly laugh before telling everyone the story about the raccoons in the kitchen. "Here's what happened," Will drew everyone in with his natural flare for spinning a tale, "Annie left the kitchen window cracked open and the coon family that lives underneath the barn decided to…" A few minutes later everyone was hooting and hollering around—at my expense, of course.

It wasn't long until the guests went back for second helpings of the delicious homemade food and Will's friend, Ricky, started tuning up his fiddle. I overheard Will talking to Bob at the far edge of the porch.

Will asked, "What are your intentions concerning Annie?"

I suppressed a moan.

"I plan to ask for her hand in marriage," Bob responded.

I silently gasped.

"Is that so?" Will pulled out his Mail Pouch tobacco and slid a pinch into his jaw. "Just so ya know, Bob, I'll be keepin' my eyes on ya and ya best treat her right or you'll have me to deal with."

"Yes, sir," Bob replied respectfully.

"Do ya plan on setting up a veterinarian shop in Erma's old clinic? You know, run it like she used to do and take time to help the poor folks around these parts."

"Yes, at least part-time, sir."

"That's good. Ya know I watched Annie stitch up old Sparky one time and she was as jumpy as a cockroach in a fryin' pan."

"Who is Sparky?" Bob asked.

"Sparky," Will explained, "is Sam's dog. The little fella has an optimistic sort of personality—a mighty pleasant disposition."

"Did Sparky heal up okay?"

"Yep," Will admitted, "he's doin' just fine, but I could tell when Annie was sewing up his cut that she was queasy. She didn't admit it though."

"Annie gets a little squeamish when it comes to certain things," Bob confirmed.

"That's for sure. She doesn't care too much for ticks." Will turned and looked at him straight in the eye. "Are ya prepared to yank a tick off of one of Hank's hairy balls should the occasion arise?"

Bob didn't falter. "Absolutely, sir."

"Good." Will teased, "Of course, she hasn't consented to marry ya, so I might not have anything to worry 'bout anyway."

Bob hesitated and bit his lip. "Very true, sir."

Finally, Will kindly uttered, "Ya appear to be a fine fella—considering you're from New York and a city-slicker." I saw his mouth intentionally twitch up at one corner.

"Thank you, sir," Bob gave a polite nod of his head.

I ducked around the side of the house, so they wouldn't realize I had been eavesdropping, and let myself in the kitchen door.

I struck up a conversation with Chloe. "Thank you very much for sprucing up this old house."

"No problem," she assured. "We'd love to see you at

Sunday services sometime."

"What time do they start?" I asked.

"At 10:00 on Sunday the choir starts singing."

"Oh?" I was thinking about Bob and Will's conversation that I had purposely overheard. *"Marriage?"* I corralled my thoughts and tried to focus on Chloe.

Bob suddenly appeared by my side, grabbed my hand and whispered in my ear, "Can we go outside? There's something I want to ask you."

"Sure."

My attention turned back to Chloe. "I'll talk to you in a little while, Chloe. Thanks again for everything."

Bob ushered me around to the side of the dilapidated building and stopped beside the drooping clusters of elderberries that were leaning against the wooden wall.

"Annie, I'm in love with you," he held both of my hands in his, "will you marry me?"

I felt my eyes widened. I took a deep breath. I needed time to think. *"He definitely tickles my fancy."* I nodded, then shook my head, and then nodded again. *"Great, he must think I'm a moron."* I wordlessly reasoned before blurting out, "We have a couple of things we should clear up first."

"Okay," he shifted his weight in anticipation, "like what?"

"What is your favorite Little Debbie snack?"

"Little Debbie snack?" Bob echoed, not bothering to mask his confusion.

"Yes."

"Well, I guess I would say Zebra Cakes."

"Oh..."

Bob's head tilted questioningly, "Is this a problem?"

"Kinda," I admitted, "Zebra Cakes are my favorite too."

"Annie," he bit his lip, "I know this is a huge decision, but I am in love with you. I will always love you and I will make a fine husband."

"I know. I love you too, Bob. It's just that I'm not sure I'm ready to share my Little Debbie Cakes with anyone," I added as an afterthought, "or my Twix bars."

"Okay," he inhaled then exhaled slowly, "what if I promise not to eat any of your Zebra Cakes or Twix bars?"

"I know I sound like a lunatic, Bob, but Pearl and Will have been having battles over their Little Debbie Cakes and I don't want to feel like I have to hide them from you in the dishwasher."

"You don't own a dishwasher, Annie."

"That is so true," I said wistfully. "You must think I'm crazy."

"I do," he teasingly responded, "so, will you marry me?"

"Yes," I smiled, "I will be honored to be your wife."

I must admit that his kiss made my knees weaken and my heart flutter. When we disengaged from the warm embrace I asked him, "When do you want to get married?"

"Right now."

My heart was pounding so hard I didn't hear anything else—not the music that played in the front yard, not the laughter reverberating from the kitchen, not even the squeals of delight coming from Buster as he rolled around in the grass with Hank. Eventually, I did respond, "Don't we need to fill out paperwork and obtain a marriage license, and..."

Bob interjected, "I took the liberty of securing a marriage license, in case you agreed, and the rest can be taken care of next week." He wiggled his eyebrows mischievously.

I explored his warm hazel eyes and his lively smile that would melt any woman's heart. "Alrighty then, handsome.

Let's get hitched."

I couldn't believe it but, at that very moment, a large white feather sailed, gliding harmoniously, down from the heavens. I reached up and captured it in my hand.

"This is a good omen, Bob," I assured him with conviction.

So, you may be wondering, "Did she actually get married wearing a bright orange carroty-colored dress?"

I sure enough did.

Bob even borrowed Hank's tie for the ceremony.

Then my old friend, who talks to angels, presented me to my groom whilst the protective light shone down on us, and down upon the whole vast yellow and crimson-covered mountaintop—in God's blessed country.

"We cannot pass our guardian angel's bounds,
resigned or sullen, he will hear our sighs."
– Saint Augustine

A Note from the Author

As the Angels of the Appalachians trilogy comes to an end, I feel a hint of sadness to let the glorious people that I loved long ago leave me again. Because when I am writing about them, and sharing the knowledge and stories they bestowed to me, I feel as if we are still closely connected. It is as though they have never left me.

Erma, Ida, Will, Pearl, Tessy and even Hank have long since passed on over to the sweet by and by, but in my mind's eye I can see them as though we were together only yesterday. These are the characters that affected my life. These are the people who taught me about love and sacrifice. These kind folks made me realize that it is small, insignificant moments that make up a lifetime. It is the joy and sorrows, the victories and defeats, the pride and shame, and the hope and despair that mold each of us as we navigate through our voyage.

To this day, I still dress in my best, slide on my rubber boots, and take the path up the muddy mountain to Beane Cemetery to visit my friends. With bouquets of wildflowers in my hand, I sing "Way Over Yonder" to them, I reminisce about their excursions, and I express my gratitude to them for being a vibrant part of my life.

The collage of experiences that I write about brings me joy as I acutely appreciate the wisdom my friends imparted to me. Thanks to the tales of my beloved comrades, and the adventures we shared, I understand the importance of faith and the significance of acts of kindness. These are the ideals that are forever imprinted in my mind. And of course, the knowledge that not only do angels walk amongst us, but that angels are always watching over us—

their protective light will shine down on us as we stumble and fumble through this splendid journey we call life.

Historical Notes and References

{{}}

The **Elkhorn Flood** that took place in 1901 in West Virginia entirely wiped out whole towns. Will was lucky to survive. There were hundreds of lives lost and millions in property destroyed as several villages were swept away, their inhabitants drowned in some instances with scarcely an escape. It was the most dreadful catastrophe in the State's history, at that time.

One newspaper reported: The sun rose this morning upon a scene of the utmost desolation. In every direction nothing is seen but evidences of wreck and ruin. The awful downpour of Friday and Saturday has caused a tremendous property loss that runs well into the millions. The loss of life, while not so great as at first reported, will number over 100 and it will be days before all the missing can be accounted for. The disaster began with a heavy rainstorm Friday afternoon, sweeping away bridges and destroying miles of railway track foundations. The people then felt no alarm, but Saturday night the storm came on again with greater intensity and shortly after midnight the elements seemed to be let loose. Thunder roared, lightning flashed and the rain came down in torrents.

The topography of the country is hilly. In the valleys are several coal mining settlements and in short order the floods that poured down upon them swept the houses and their inmates to wreck and death. The town of Keystone, a flourishing little village, was swept out of existence. The coal mines in the vicinity were destroyed and the men on guard drowned. Twenty-eight miles of railroad track and everything in its path was swept away. The loss to the Norfolk & Eastern railway is enormous. The flood came down suddenly Saturday morning on Shakrege and in an hour the little village was underneath six feet of water and nearly every one living there was killed. The big Van Dyke farm was destroyed and the entire family Van Dyke father, mother and four children Van Dyke were drowned.

The fury of the storm was without a parallel in the history of the State. All day yesterday the missing turned up. This morning forty bodies had been recovered. Pathetic and tragic scenes were numerous. Hundreds are homeless and the suffering among the living today is frightful. Many are on the brink of starvation.

The storm swept district covers an area of thirty miles and the wreck will be old before the number of lives sacrificed can be positively ascertained. It is known, however, that the property loss in the Elkhorn district will be considerably more than $2,000,000. Governor White said he fears the death list of the Elkhorn flood will be over 1000 and possibly reach 2000.

http://www.gendisasters.com/west-virginia/2295/bluefield%2C-wv-elkhorn-creek-flood%2C-jun-1901

{{}}

The **Lost Battalion** is the name given to nine companies of the United States 77th Division, roughly 554 men, isolated by German forces during World War I after an American attack in the Argonne Forest in October 1918.

Roughly 197 were killed in action and approximately 150 missing or taken prisoner before 194 remaining men were rescued. Major Charles Whittlesey led them. On October 2, the division quickly advanced into the Argonne, under the belief that French forces were supporting the left flank and two American units were supporting the right flank. Unknown to Whittlesey's unit, the French advance had been stalled. Without this knowledge, the Americans had moved beyond the rest of the allied line and found themselves completely cut off and surrounded by German forces. For the next several days, suffering heavy losses, the men of the division were forced to fight off several attacks by the Germans, who saw the small American units as a threat to their whole line.

The battalion suffered many hardships. Food was short, and water was available only by crawling under fire to a nearby stream. Ammunition ran low. Communications were also a problem, and at times shells from their own artillery would bombard them. As every runner dispatched by Whittlesey either became lost or ran into German patrols, carrier pigeons became the only method of communicating with headquarters. In a famous incident on October 4 inaccurate coordinates were delivered by one of the pigeons and the unit was subjected to "friendly fire." Another pigeon named Cher Ami saved the unit.

Despite this, they held their ground and caused enough of a distraction for other allied units to break through the German lines, which forced the Germans to retreat.

http://military.wikia.com/wiki/Lost_Battalion_(World_War_I)

{{}}

For years Will was employed as a Mason, aiding in the construction of the **West Virginia State Capitol**. The capitol was previously located in downtown Charleston from 1885 until it burned down on January 3,1921. It then moved to what was called the "Pasteboard Capitol" from 1921 until March of 1927, when it burned to the ground leaving many of the departments of state homeless once more.

The present Capitol took eight years to complete at a cost of just under $10 million. The 293-foot gold atop the capitol is five feet higher than the dome of the United States Capitol. The dome is layered in copper, and covered with gold leaf. The beautiful golden-domed structure has two biblical inscriptions carved in stone tablets on the north and south bases of the Capitol dome. On the north side it states, "Wisdom is the principle thing. Therefore, get wisdom. And with all of thy getting, get understanding." The south side inscription conveys the following message: "Happy is the man that findeth wisdom and getteth understanding."

http://www.generalservices.wv.gov/history-of-the capitol/Pages/default.aspx

{{}}

Throughout the years, West Virginia has suffered many tragedies that left hundreds of workers injured or dead. These tragedies are the result of disasters occurring in our coal mines, on our railroads and at industrial facilities like the **Hawks Nest Tunnel** incident. This disaster became one of the worst industrial tragedies in the history of the United States and Will believed he was saved from this tragedy due to the intervention of his guardian angel.

Drilled through three miles of solid rock, the Hawks Nest Tunnel is a major hydroelectric water diversion tunnel and an engineering marvel. Largely constructed between 1930 and 1932, the project engaged almost 5,000 workers, consisting of local men and a majority of migrant workers. The tunnel was part of a complex to generate power for Union electro-metallurgical plant in nearby Alloy. It was the largest construction project that had been licensed to that time in West Virginia, and it became the site of one of the worst industrial tragedies in the history of the United States.

In all, 2,982 men worked underground drilling and blasting. Only 40 percent of the underground work force worked more than two months and only 20 percent worked more than six months. Silicosis afflicted an astonishingly high proportion of this short-tenured work force. Silicosis, a progressive fibrosis of the lungs caused by inhaling pulverized silica dioxide, was a recognized hazard in hard rock mining and in granite sheds. Because the Hawks Nest Tunnel was licensed as a civil engineering project, even the modest forms of safety enforcement then available to miners did not apply.

The combination of large work crews drilling and blasting in underground confined spaces, poor ventilation, lack of dust control and of personal breathing protection, and seams of exceptionally pure silica combined to create a man-made disaster. In less than two years after groundbreaking in April 1930, young men succumbed to acute silicosis. Many of the workers eventually died.
https://www.wvencyclopedia.org/articles/338

The **Silver Bridge**, so-called by Point Pleasant-area residents viewing its silvery aluminum paint for the first time, was designed by J.E. Greiner Company and built by Gallia County Ohio River Bridge Company (later West Virginia-Ohio Bridge Company) and its subcontractor, U.S. Steel's American Bridge Company. A two-lane, 1760-foot-long eye bar suspension bridge with a 700-foot main span 102 feet above the bottom of the Ohio River channel and two 380-foot anchor spans, it was completed in one year, opening to traffic on Memorial Day 1928.

Although the original design had called for conventional wire cables, an eye bar chain design—bid as an alternate—came in at a lower price. The bridge was described in the June 20, 1929 *Engineering News Record* as "the first of its type in the United States." Unlike three chain-link suspension bridges at Pittsburgh and others throughout the world, particularly in Europe, the Silver Bridge's anchorages were, according to the magazine, "unique (in their) use of heat-treated eye bar chains, portions of which form parts of the top chords of the stiffening trusses." In this arrangement, each chain link consisted of a pair of bone-shaped 2x12-inch bars, varying in length from 45 to 55 feet by their position on the bridge, with 11-inch-diameter pins connecting the links through the "eyes" at the ends of the bars. These chains constituted the upper chord to a Warren-type stiffening truss in the seven panels of each side span and 12 panels of the center span.

Perhaps ominously, the *Engineering News Record* article also noted the fact that it was not possible to make "any adjustments in the chains, hangers or trusses after erection."

At 5 p.m. on December 15, 1967, eyewitnesses recall, there was a loud gunshot-like noise and, "folding like a deck of cards" in less than 20 seconds, the entire 1460-foot suspended portion of the Silver Bridge collapsed into the river, taking with it 32 vehicles and 46 victims, including two whose bodies were never found.

On April 6, 1971, the Safety Board finally issued its determination of the cause of the collapse—"a cleavage fracture in the lower limb of the eye of eye bar 330 at joint C13N of the north eye bar suspension chain in the Ohio side span. The fracture was caused by the development of a critical-size flaw over the 40-year life of the structure as the result of the joint action of stress corrosion and corrosion fatigue."

http://www.transportation.wv.gov/highways/bridge_facts/Modern-Bridges/Pages/Silver.aspx

{{}}

Will's tale about the **Mothman** is recorded in a book written by John Keel in 1975 entitled *The Mothman Prophecies.* The book relates Keel's accounts of his investigation into alleged sightings of a large, winged creature called Mothman in the vicinity of Point Pleasant, West Virginia, during 1966 and 1967. It combines these accounts with his theories about UFOs and various supernatural phenomena, ultimately connecting them to the collapse of the Silver Bridge across the Ohio River on December 15, 1967. Official investigations in 1971 determined the bridge collapse was caused by stress corrosion cracking in an eye bar in a suspension chain.

The book was the inspiration for the 2002 film of the same name, starring Richard Gere.

{{}}

On November 14, 1970, a chartered jet carrying most of the **Marshall University** football team clipped a stand of trees and crashed into a hillside just two miles from the Tri-State Airport in Kenova, West Virginia. The team was returning from that day's game, a 17-14 loss to East Carolina University. Thirty-seven Marshall football players were aboard the plane, along with the team's coach, its doctors, the university athletic director and 25 team boosters, and some of Huntington, West Virginia's most prominent citizens who had traveled to North Carolina to cheer on the Thundering Herd. "The whole fabric," a citizen of Huntington wrote later, "the whole heart of the town was aboard."

The crash was just the most tragic in a string of unfortunate events that had befallen the Marshall football team since about 1960. The university stadium, which hadn't been renovated since before World War II, was condemned in 1962. From the last game of the 1966 season to midway through the 1969 season, the team hadn't won any games. Making matters worse, the NCAA had suspended Marshall for more than 100 recruiting violations. However, Marshall seemed to be getting back on track. It had fired the dishonest coaches, built a new Astroturf field and started winning games again. The

Thundering Herd had lost a squeaker to East Carolina on the 14th, and was looking forward to a promising season the next year.

For Huntington, the plane crash was "like the Kennedy assassination," one citizen remembers. "Everybody knows where they were and what they were doing when they heard the news." The town immediately went into mourning. Shops and government offices closed; businesses on the town's main street draped their windows in black bunting. The university held a memorial service in the stadium the next day and cancelled Monday's classes. There were so many funerals that they had to be spread out over several weeks. In perhaps the saddest ceremony of all, six players whose remains couldn't be identified were buried together in Spring Hill Cemetery, on a hill overlooking their university.

http://www.history.com/this-day-in-history/plane-crash-devastates-marshall-university

In 2006 the movie *We Are Marshall* was released. It is based on the story of the Marshall University football team tragedy and stars Matthew McConaughey, Matthew Fox, and Anthony Mackie.

{{}}

The Peanut Shoppe has been a tradition for over 60 years in Charleston, West Virginia. The shop is located at 126 Capitol Street, which is across from the Kanawha County Public Library. The scent of fresh, handmade caramels, pulled creams, hot roasted cashews and Spanish nuts will make your mouth water when you walk past the little shop. The nuts are toasted in their shells onsite using an antique planter's gas-burning roaster. It was Pearl's favorite place to shop.

{{}}

While living in Huntington, West Virginia, Will frequented a place called **Stewart's Original Hotdogs**. The famous hotdog stand began in 1932, when the husband and wife team of John Louis and Gertrude Mandt opened the first drive-in restaurant in Huntington. They purchased a little piece of land at 2445 Fifth Avenue and built, at a cost of $1,750, a tiny orange building that still stands today. The menu consisted of only two items: Stewart's Root Beer and popcorn. Sales for the first day totaled an unimpressive 50 cents.

Hoping to do better the next year, they added hotdogs to the menu, complete with Gertrude's mouthwatering chili sauce. Today, the business and the little orange building are still going strong. Her great grandson, John Mandt Jr., the drive-in's fourth generation owner, closely guards Gertrude's secret recipe, which is still used today.

{{}}

Will first met Erma when he worked at Luna Park. J. B. Crowley built **Luna Park** in 1912 on the north bank of the Kanawha River in Charleston. The amusement park occupied seven acres on what had been a three-hole golf course. At the main entrance on Park Avenue stood a large wooden fence with two flag topped spires. Behind the fence, a footbridge led to level ground where park goers could ride

126

the Royal Giant Dips Coaster, a merry-go-round, and a Ferris wheel; play games of chance and skill on the midway; and picnic under shade trees. People walked to the park or rode streetcars. Excursion boats from Gallipolis, Ohio and Point Pleasant, West Virginia stopped to let off passengers. On May 5, 1923, a fire started by welders working on a new swimming pool destroyed most of the park. Although Luna's owners announced that they would rebuild, the park never reopened.

http://www.wvencyclopedia.org/articles/1465

{{}}

Some of Will's jokes can be found in a book called *More Laughter in Appalachia (Southern Mountain Humor)* by Loyal Jones and Billy Edd Wheeler, August House Publishers, Inc., 1995.

{{}}

Thank ya for reading *Will's Journey*.

I sincerely hope you enjoyed *Will's Journey*. I would greatly appreciate your opinion with an honest review on Amazon.com or Goodreads.com.

First and foremost, I'm always looking to grow and improve as a writer. It is reassuring to hear what works, as well as to receive constructive feedback on what should be improved. Secondly, proceeds earned from this book are donated to the Monroe County Humane Society, and the animals can always use your help.

Best regards,
Deanna Edens

35353564R00083

Made in the USA
Columbia, SC
20 November 2018